OF HUMAN CLAY

Aimee Wise

Aimee Wise (signature)

i

Publisher: Aimee Wise

Printed in the United States of America.

First soft cover edition published August 2013.

The author wishes to thank the following people who contributed to this book:

Medical Mission Sisters Archives for their photos on pages 103, 138, 154.

The SMM Dutch Archives for the eulogy excerpts on page 297.

Dr. Thomas Wagner, Technische Universität München, for the use of his photo of Phalombe Church, page 147.

Daniel Alvarez/Shutterstock.com for the photo of the hyena, page 156.

The remainder of the photos belong to the author or her family. The author apologizes for the poor quality of many of them; they were taken with unsophisticated cameras and are over forty years old.

Cover design and interior layout by Rebecca Shaw.

THIS BOOK IS DEDICATED TO:

Gerard

Ndimakukonda pano ndi nthawi zonse.

ACKNOWLEDGMENTS

My past illusion that a book is the sole creation of one author has been completely sacked. This published memoir has been kneaded into its present shape by so many people, I'm embarrassed to be the only name on the cover.

I want to acknowledge the multitude of family, friends, and professionals who all contributed in some way to this book's existence:

My beloved parents, Tom and Ann; my treasured siblings: Dot Bruno, Gina Clay, Ronnie McCullion and Mike McCullion; my three deceased brothers Tom, Dan, and John McCullion; and my extended clan, all of us bound together by unconditional love.

My older brother, Dan, and his wife, Janice, who gifted me a diary each year of my adolescence, and my mother, who preserved twelve years of letters and audiotapes I sent home.

Mother Anna Dengel, MD, and her community of Medical Mission Sisters, who are a healing presence in our wounded world. I admire their lives. Were it possible, I would wash the feet of each of those women.

My dear companions in the Pilot Project: Norma, Pat, Flora, and Yoli.

The warm-hearted people of Malawi, who still today lack the essentials of clean water, adequate food, education, healthcare, and the means to a humane livelihood.

Gerard, who poured out his beautiful soul into thousands of words on countless onionskin pages, so lyrical they deserve a book of their own.

The members of my two talented and generous Atlanta writing groups, who nudged me into a better writer over many months: Angela Durden,

Chuck Clark, Chuck Johnson, Greta Reed, Jedwin Smith, Jim Butorac, Marilyn Berman, Rebecca Ewing, Ron Aiken, Sandie Webb, and William Whitson.

My much-loved friends and family, who listened and supported me while I wrote this book and read drafts, did editing, and gave valuable suggestions: Angelika Pohl, Chris Frost, Debee Di Minichi, Gabrielle Guyton-Emiston, Gail Livingston, Greta Reed, Marilyn Berman, Marni Hydrusko, Ronnie McCullion, Sandy Campanella, and Zach Cable.

The professionals who guided me through the writing and publishing maze: Cynthia Blakeley, my editor, for her wise thoughtfulness and invitation to dig deeper, and Rebecca Shaw, graphic designer, who worked patiently and generously to transform my rough manuscript into a real book. Deborah Gonzalez, Esq. for wise legal counsel. Chris Frost, designer, for her invaluable artistic input on the cover. Tom Whitfield, whose suggestions after reading two drafts were invaluable, and Angela Durden and Kim Green, who generously shared their writing/publishing experience with me. Finally, Jedwin Smith, who lovingly gifted me with a review.

Sister Jane Gates and Annaig Boyer, the Medical Mission Sisters' archivists who gave me access to the community's records, and Sister Estelle DeMers. Their generous sharing of time and information allowed me to better understand the Pilot Project and my past.

My three grown and precious children: Katherine Robeson and her husband Ken, Suzanne Wise, and Michael Wise. There was no better motivation to bring it to completion than their unswerving interest.

My five grandchildren: Lauren, Brian, Patrick, Zachary, and Justin, who know I adore them and hope they understand from *my* story that the mistakes of youth are part of their journey to adulthood.

They are not alone.

TABLE OF CONTENTS

PREFACE

*W*hat is that red box?

Rummaging through a bedroom closet in 2010, I noticed a large cardboard container pushed far back on one of the shelves. *Odd not to remember that it was there.*

Retrieved from the dark recess, the box now sat beside me on the carpet. Bothered by my growing forgetfulness and feeling a child's curiosity, I lifted the lid.

Inside was a jumble of letters and journals, photos and tapes from when I lived in Africa in my twenties.

Yellowed pages scribbled by the light of a kerosene lamp told of a towering bonfire urged on by pounding drums in Tengani village. The fire ate up the dark, outlined thatched roofs, and glistened bodies dancing in rhythm with the flames.

A few faded photos spilled from a bulging envelope: scenes of the Zambezi River, a baobab tree, villagers butchering a hippo.

The act of opening that box shattered my day's agenda and propelled me back into Malawi of the 1970s. The photos resurrected a young, dark-haired woman whom I barely recognized. Yet as chambered memories spiraled open, I knew her—once again.

Digging through those forgotten relics over many months, I discovered that the "Africa story" I told myself and others was an unconscious revision of the true events.

CHAPTER ONE

MAY 9, 1971

The creaks and moans of the rusty metal stairs rolling away from the plane's doorway are proof there's no further escape from this lamentable journey.

As the VC10 rattles in its ascent, I stare in disbelief at the dissolving forms below. An invisible thief is stealing away the airport and the road, the people and places I love.

As the engines shift into a cruising hum, the elderly Indian beside me turns and cups his body toward me. Tilting his head to see me better, he peers through wire glasses perched midway down his nose—a Mahatma Gandhi clone.

"So, tell me, young lady of the tears—why are you leaving Malawi?"

Glancing into his concerned eyes, I'm afraid to speak lest my emotional turmoil burst through the wall I've erected to survive this trip. I barely managed to hold myself together at the tiny Chileka airport during the good-byes to my friends—and to Gerard.

Please don't probe, I think. *I can't talk now.*

The old gentleman waits, expectant.

What to do? He is being so kind, so sympathetic.

"Well . . . I am returning home . . . to the United States . . . " A sob breaks through. "But I don't want to leave."

He pats my hand, "There there, young one."

His tender listening invites more feelings.

"I've wanted to live and work in Africa since I was a young girl, but now—after only a year and a half—I have to go home."

His face registers worry. "Are you sick, my dear? Did you pick up one of our nasty diseases? It happens often with foreigners."

"No . . . only sick in my heart."

"Ah, that's the hardest to heal. There are no medicines for it—only time."

"I'll never recover from this. My life's a failure. I've brought shame on myself." I look away out the window, unable to hold back the choking sounds coming from my throat.

While I struggle for control, he sits quietly for a moment, then observes, "But you are so young and, I think, a good person. What could you have done to have such bad feelings about yourself, your life?"

Crumpling my wet tissue, I sniffle, "You are very kind . . . but it is too long a story . . . and difficult to explain to anyone."

"Well, my child, we have a long ride ahead. Why not start at the beginning and tell me what has brought you to this sad departure?"

*

Start at the beginning? When was that?

Is it ever possible to know the origin of any consequence? We are shaped by influences stretching back over our lives, to our birth family, to our sensory perceptions in the womb, to our ancestors who bequeathed us their genetic inclinations.

The beginning? Was it the meeting with the bishop . . . or my decision to join the mobile health team in the Lower Shire Plain . . . or even earlier, in the language and culture course where I met Gerard?

No, the roots of this day go back further still.

He said we have time.

"My name is Aimee—Sister Aimee—and I need to take you as far back as my birth, twenty-nine years ago. Is that okay?"

He wobbles his gray head, a slight smile on his crinkled face. "Yes, that is a *very* long time indeed. But I am here listening, so just begin."

Over the following hours, while the plane flew over the darkening African continent, its jet stream marking our passage, I told Mr. Mehta my story.

CHAPTER TWO

DUTIFUL DAUGHTER

Imagine my parents, Tom and Ann, clinging to each other during those frightening winter months after the 1941 attack on Pearl Harbor. Perhaps on one of those cold February nights, surrendering fear to passion, they conceived their first daughter, Annamarie. On November 5, 1942, I entered life as a "war baby," a somber epithet for seven pounds of peaceful new life.

The joy of my arrival tempered the radio's jarring words of invasions and lost lives flooding into our inner-city rowhouse wedged between identical others on a long Philadelphia street.

Returning each night from his job as a truck driver, my dad settled himself in the doily-draped armchair of the tiny living room. Nestling me in his tired arms, he'd croon Irish lullabies—the hooks on which he hung his heart: "Over in Killarney," "When Irish Eyes are Smiling," or "Who Threw the Overalls in Mrs. Murphy's Chowder."

My aproned mom called my older brothers from their dodgeball game in the street outside for their nightly chore of setting the table for supper. Meat, potatoes, and overcooked vegetables were the usual fare, unless it was a Catholic tomato soup and canned tuna Friday.

My brothers, ten and eight when I was born, were the sons of my father and his first wife, who died when the boys were just four and two. Sadly, the motherless toddlers were separated, and cared for by different grandmothers for several years until their father remarried. Imagine the joy for them to be together again with him, with a new mother, and the novelty of a female baby in the house. Racing in from school each day, their shirts askew, their hair sweaty and awry, they wrangled over who would hold me first. "Mom, it's my turn to hold the baby," declared Tommy. The younger Danny fussed, "Not fair, you got to hold her this morning." The squabble over me went back and forth.

My family's love has backlit my entire life. It has been an ever-present safety net, a warm security blanket wrapped around me in times of need.

My early family.

Both my parents were Catholic and raised us children in their traditional faith, although I remember that my feisty Irish grandmother had an imposing picture of FDR on her kitchen wall that dwarfed the one of Jesus. Politics and religion were inseparable for her, especially when it came to equality for downtrodden people like herself. She passed on that sensitivity toward inequity to me.

Her Irish husband was a Pennsylvania coal miner who sang with the Anthracite Miner's Glee Club. A treasured photo captures him and his fellow singers dressed in their Sunday suits, fedoras in hand, posed in front of the club banner. No smiles lit their faces; they knew the dangerous mines awaited them the next day.

My clan descended from hardworking, heavy-drinking, uneducated Irish with a dash of German and Lithuanian on my mom's maternal side to spice the lineage. My mother was the only child of divorced parents and I know little of her family history, except for a story of her soldier grandfather, who was a bigamist. Hearing that tidbit when I was young, I assumed he had been someone important.

In the late 1940s the postwar recovery fueled a better salary for my dad. Since the skinny rowhouse bulged with our growing family, my parents joined the white flight to the suburbs triggered by racial tensions disrupting the City of Brotherly Love. We piled into the old Packard for an hour's drive to a house with a sprawling yard in suburban Havertown. Tommy and Danny were seventeen and fifteen, I was seven, my sister Dorothy three. Counting the baby in Mom's belly—a boy to be named John—Dad had five kids to support. Three more children: Regina, Veronica, and Michael came along later to fill the new house and add to his roll of dependants.

My child's eyes perceived that second residence as a mansion, although a later visit revealed a much smaller house than the one I'd carried in my mental wallet. That second home and its neighborhood stood like a mother, her boundaries a protective embrace against the ugly side of humanity in the world beyond. I lived in ignorance of racism, sexual abuse, homophobia, drugs —social issues sadly familiar to me in my adult years.

Havertown House.

Mornings were harried in our "mansion," with only one bathroom. Dad had first rights, then we kids filed in, each claiming a station: one brushed teeth at the sink, another used the toilet, while the third took a quick bath.

Unlike Sunday mornings when Dad cooked a sumptuous meal of eggs, scrapple and bacon, and his masterful fried potatoes, our weekday breakfast was a hasty bowl of cereal followed by the shuffle of bodies pulling jackets from the closet, searching for misplaced schoolbooks, and grabbing metal lunch boxes from the kitchen.

In my early teens, I usually slipped off to 7:00 a.m. Mass at the nearby parish church. A fifteen-minute walk brought me to the soaring facade of Annunciation of the Blessed Virgin Mary Church, with its massive stained-glass window. The impressive gray stone structure stood guard on the main street through Havertown. I trusted in its constant protection. Drawn to all things religious, I loved starting the day with the peaceful Mass rituals, the priest's familiar Latin singsong, and sharing the shadowed pews with a few elderly women. Returning home, I'd grab breakfast and rush out with my siblings, all earlier calm lost.

After we left for school Mom cared for the youngest ones at home, washed piles of laundry, ironed, cleaned, and prepared dinner. The family budget and her cooking experience confined us to simple, repetitive meals. Sometimes Mom bought a steak just for my father, teaching us to be grateful for his role as the family's provider. We watched him from our chairs around the table, salivating as he savored the meat, drops of its juice wetting his lips.

On weeknights while dinner was cooking in the kitchen and I set the table, Mom headed upstairs and changed into silk hose and a fresh housedress before Dad came home. Walking in from work Dad often grabbed her around the waist and nuzzled her neck as she stood at the stove, but Mom usually elbowed him away, embarrassed by his affectionate display in front of us children.

Many years later my modest mother confessed that she dressed and undressed in their bedroom closet so Dad wouldn't see her naked. Her shyness wasn't much of a deterrent; together they conceived eight children. Six were full term while two were grieved miscarriages.

In the evenings while Mom cleaned up after dinner or talked in subdued tones with Dad at the kitchen table, my younger siblings and I tackled homework, then plunked in front of our tiny TV and demolished a nightly bowl of corn flakes. By then my two older brothers had each joined the Marine Corps.

Many nights putting the kids to bed fell to me. Once their teeth were brushed, faces washed, and pajamas donned, I tucked the covers around them and began my special ritual. Going from bed to bed, I sang hymns to them while sliding my fingers along the soft skin of their arms and faces to make them sleepy. My favorite song, sung in my out-of-pitch voice, was "Jesus, my Lord, my God, my All."

One or the other would beg me for more "tickling," as we called it. "Rie Rie, tickle my arm sa' more. I not sleepy yet." Everyone in my family and neighborhood called me Rie or Rie-Rie, a nickname instigated by my younger sister Dorothy, who couldn't wrap her baby tongue around Annamarie.

But it wasn't only my younger siblings whose days ended on a religious note. I can picture my parents kneeling on either side of their marriage bed saying their nightly prayers. Something deep within us shifts when we humans kneel. Before I climbed into bed after my prayers, I added my own ritual of recording my daily good deeds and faults in a small notebook. It was a ledger to assess my net gain or loss in my earnest pursuit of perfection.

While I wanted to be helpful at home, numerous family duties sometimes hung like a bag of stones around my neck. Like any young girl I wanted to play with friends after school, but my mother often needed me. She relied on her oldest daughter to help, as was the tradition in many large families. My early role as second-string mother for my five younger siblings and the most popular babysitter in the neighborhood burdened me with an exaggerated sense of responsibility, a psychic thorn for much of my life.

An early experience also fueled a layer of fear beneath my sense of duty. One summer day I lost my baby sister during a family vacation.

That morning my parents had staked out our beach spot with blankets. At noon they headed back to the rented apartment for lunch, but I wanted to stay and soak up more rays to get that perfect tan for my teen body. My two-year-old sister, intently digging her way to China at the water's edge, also begged to stay.

Stretched out on the blanket, warmed by the noonday sun, I fell asleep. Sometime later Mom was frantically shaking me awake, panic in her voice: "Where's your sister?" In my foggy state I mumbled, "Uh . . . she's down by the water."

But she wasn't there.

Over the next agonizing hour my family searched along the beach for a little blond girl. I mentally wrestled with the unbearable thought that she had been carried off by a wave or kidnapped—and it was *my* fault.

After anxiously racing back and forth along the surf and among sprawled bodies and tilted umbrellas, we enlisted a lifeguard's help. He located my sister at their headquarters on the boardwalk. She had wandered down the beach crying when she couldn't find me, and a stranger had taken her to a nearby guard.

In the station, sobs of relief broke from my chest, tears brimmed on Mom's face, and we all jostled to hug a lollypop-sucking Ronnie.

Well into midlife I suffered a recurrent nightmare: I am a young girl standing on a hill that overlooks a sprinkle of summer cottages edging the ocean. A tsunami, hundreds of feet high, is rising on the horizon. Though petrified, I don't run to my parents for help; I race down toward the rapidly approaching menace, compelled to save all my siblings at play on the beach.

In later life I questioned my mother, "Why did you give me so much responsibility for the kids when I was so young?" Surprised and hurt, she replied, "But you always wanted to do it; you asked to help me. I didn't force you."

From one perspective, what Mom said was true. When I was eight, her ill and alcoholic mother came to live with us around the same time Mom's fifth child was born. Sensing her stress at having her mother reappear in her life, I went into overdrive to protect my mom in the only ways I knew as a young girl—never misbehaving and helping as much as I could.

But that worry-based sensitivity, reinforced by the Church's teachings, twisted into a perception that I had to earn love through obedience and docility. In spite of my parents' unconditional love, that early misconception took root and delayed the development of my personal autonomy.

My Havertown years from age seven through seventeen were populated with far more than parents and siblings. Relatives arrived almost every weekend. Our extended family was magnetically drawn to our motherly house, with its wide front porch, amply endowed rooms, and an unfinished basement where the guys hung out to throw darts. The stairway to the five bedrooms on the second floor had steps from both the front entrance and the back kitchen, making it a perfect racetrack for all of the boys to run up and down. Hiding in my parents' bedroom, we girls played dress-up with Mom's shoes and jewelry. The adults sat at the kitchen table drinking highballs, smoking, and discussing their worlds over penny-ante poker games.

Our house was not the only magnet; the large swing set and sliding board in the backyard enticed all the neighborhood kids as well as the cousins. The grass around the area was worn bare from the scuffing of worn school oxfords and Keds.

One spring my father consulted a lawn service about growing grass on our corner property. When the man saw the swarm of kids in our yard, he bluntly asked, "Sir, do you want a lawn, or do you want kids? You can't have both." Dad chose the kids.

My childhood was like a sardine can crammed with my family, relatives, neighbors, and school playmates. People filled my days—and even my nights. Well after bedtime my younger siblings often wandered into my narrow twin bed, leaving me no space to turn over. The final straw came one morning when I felt my younger brother, Johnny, lying upside down alongside me—his foot resting on my chin.

Never lonely growing up, I often craved time alone. What a joy to escape to my bedroom to read, all sense of time and place lost as I became Jo in *Eight Cousins* or Nancy Drew, the schoolgirl sleuth. Immersed in another existence, I rarely heard my mother calling me to help.

Those Havertown years were a Camelot period for my family. My parents and close-knit relatives were healthy, their children thriving, their incomes sufficient for a simple, middle-class life—and the country was at peace.

There were times when my frustrated mother used a hairbrush as a spanking tool or my tired father threatened us into submission by pulling off his belt. Such occasional physical punishment was normal in our neighborhood during that era, and I still wince when recalling Mom's icy silence if she was angry. Yet those moments were insignificant against the truth of my mother and father as loving and beloved.

My younger siblings experienced different, less relaxed parents as Dad aged and became increasingly disabled from a failing heart, and Mom juggled an outside job to bring in money, along with all the other demands on her time and energy.

In my mature years I understood my parents as the good—and flawed—individuals they were: my father's homophobia, which caused him to reject my gay younger brother, Johnny, and my mother's depression in the years after Dad's death. He had adored her and when she lost her soulmate at fifty, she had three teens still at home and little income. Because of glimpses I gained from rare conversational cracks in the wall Mom had erected about her past, I suspect that, in her aloneness after my father's death, her own unresolved, abusive childhood returned to haunt her.

CHAPTER THREE

MASS AND MARTYRS

The Catholic faith, our family's bedrock, molded my childhood and adolescence. Since the Church taught that an unbaptized baby who died was condemned to Limbo for eternity, my parents hurried me to the baptismal font in my first weeks.

Receiving the sacraments was de rigueur for all Catholics. After my First Confession and First Communion at age seven, I lined up at the altar railing for the sacrament of Confirmation when I was twelve. In that ritual, the presiding bishop lightly slapped each child's cheek, a reminder to be a strong Catholic, prepared to suffer even martyrdom for one's faith. At thirteen, I wrote in my diary:

> At Mass, I told God that if he wanted to send me any crosses to bear, even death, I was ready.

While my peers swooned over TV personalities, I could have started a fan club for martyrs. I knew the names and stories of which ones were roasted to death, shot with arrows, or thrown over cliffs.

Though martyrdom lost its appeal as I aged, attraction to heroic suffering remained a psychic strand woven through my life. Tragic heroines like Kristin Lavransdatter in Sigrid Undset's novel, or the widowed Jackie Kennedy, became my touchstones. While naturally inclined to be caring, my ego found gratification in sacrificing my needs or wants for others. Catholicism's ascetic history, coupled with my female upbringing, abetted what was an unbalanced tendency in me. Yet it wasn't a sense of inferiority; rather, in my own inner drama, selflessness made me feel noble.

The parish church was my second home, and its spiritual aura resonated in me from an early age. I loved the serene atmosphere and religious rituals: reciting the Mass prayers in my small Latin missal, smelling the waves of incense, receiving Holy Communion with eyes closed, hands joined in reverence.

One Sunday afternoon I wrote in my adolescent diary:

> Around communion, I suddenly had a strange feeling. I always have an excited feeling in my heart, but I don't know if it's from going to receive Jesus, or getting up in front of people to walk down the aisle.

My brothers' passion for collecting baseball cards was mirrored in my collection of holy cards. These were typically distributed at funerals or

handed out by the nuns as rewards for good behavior. I stored mine in an old cardboard cigar box on my bedroom vanity table and studied each image of Jesus, Mary, and the saints. Even today, if I chance to be in a religious bookstore where cellophane-wrapped holy cards hang from display hooks, I know the names of all the saints from their traditional depictions.

Friends and I walked to our parish church for Confession on Saturdays to ensure our souls were without sin before receiving Communion the next day. My parochial school sat beside the church, tightly linking education and faith throughout my childhood.

Each school year culminated in a May procession in honor of the Blessed Mother. All the students dressed in white: boys in short pants with shirts, ties, and jackets; girls in the frilliest, most bouffant dresses and veils their mothers could find. After assembling in the church, a chain of angelic-looking children, heads bowed, hands together, moved out onto the sidewalk and walked around the block. Passing motorists gawked. My father, camera in hand, would entreat me to look up at him, but the nuns told us to keep our eyes down. Those annual rituals were my first conflict in obedience—should I obey the nuns or my father? That tension was the first of many fine cracks in my automatic response to authority figures. My readiness to question and challenge those with title or rank came much later—and too late.

The staff of nuns in each grade taught about the missions in foreign places like Africa and China, where a degree of poverty and suffering existed that was inconceivable in my insular world. Those images set fire to my impressionable imagination. I searched for fallen change in the couch cushions and on the street to drop in the school mission boxes. Mom let me dig in the bottom of her pocketbooks among crumpled tissues for stray coins.

My childhood awareness of the world's inequities stirred a sense of compassion in me that was tinged with the excitement of exotic lands. I longed for a bigger stage than my neighborhood, envisioned myself as Joan of Arc, sword in hand, ready to slay the evils of disease and misery in distant places.

Several diary entries written during my years from thirteen to seventeen reflect the conflicting desires of my adolescence:

Good night Dear Diary. I'm going to be a saint.

*

I watched the movie "30 Seconds over Tokyo" about Army pilots. I want to do something to help those fellows who are doing so much for us. I could join the Army Nurse Corp so I can help people and bring them happiness. I want to do something important and not just settle down and get married. I want to see life and live it.

*

I wish I could be a singer or dancer. I would love to be on stage and feel talented and beautiful.

*

At Mass, I felt the utter shortness of life. Everything seems so common. I obviously have a vocation to be a nun.

What attuned me to the ephemeral nature of existence as a young teen? It's a recurrent theme in my diaries and has persisted throughout my life; in the background of my days I hear the whoosh of sand through an hourglass.

Along with the perception of life as fleeting was an awareness of something more substantial, more essential, beneath the layers of daily activities and the "stuff" that occupied people. A sense of the sacred was a buried ore in me—and would be tested in the inescapable fires of adulthood.

While I found emotional comfort in spirituality during my adolescent years, my faith also prodded me with demanding yardsticks of virtue and grinding guilt for any imperfection.

My diaries reveal the struggle I encountered in even small decisions. I debated whether to wear my high heels to the Sears after-school modeling class with my friends and be vain, or wear my ugly school oxfords and be humble. I also worried that liking praise would deprive me of a reward in heaven.

One entry even conveyed my frustration at being human:

I was thinking about the prom coming up and how dumb boys are, and the way people act so human. I keep looking for perfection in people and things and can't find it. But it especially hurts when I find such imperfection in me.

And then this entry when I was fifteen:

> Well, Dear Diary, this year has ended and brought
> me a little closer to old age. During this year I've
> had lots of dates, but my spiritual life is being
> neglected. I'm just not as close to God as I was before,
> so I will try to do better in the coming year.

In response to my probing questions about life and why things happened as they did, my mother often chided me, "Rie, you think too much." Both of my parents had to go to work before they finished high school; my father's schooling ended after eighth grade, my mother's after tenth. Perhaps my formal education and searching mind traveled down roads my mother never considered or felt able to explore. Her comments, which I perceived as criticism, distorted my thinking. I felt flawed for not knowing, for needing to ask. My unspoken questions left me flapping like a fish on a hook. I began sharing my thoughts only with my diary or turning to God and the saints for help:

> God, please bless my work of selling the greeting
> cards I bought through the magazine offer so I can
> help Mom and Dad with money. And Jesus, please
> give me the courage to sell my cards door to door.

Trying out for the prestigious glee club in high school, I called upon the patron saint of musicians:

> Dear Saint Cecilia, if it is God's will, please let
> me make the glee club. My friends all say I have a
> terrible voice.

Even Saint Cecilia didn't have *that* much power. During the first round of tryouts, the teacher grimaced as I sang and suggested I find another club to join.

An incident when I was fifteen prompted yet another request for heavenly intervention. I had lost my pencil case, which held my favorite pen. It was silver and gold-plated and a more costly gift than anything I typically owned. I felt so irresponsible. I beseeched the saint known for finding lost things to help me.

Over the next several months I scribbled the following reminders—and reprimands—on the bottom of some of my diary pages:

> No pen, Saint Anthony.

>   *

> Saint Anthony, please don't forget about my pen.

>   *

> Good-night, dear Jesus. Would you help me find my pen?

>   *

> Saint Anthony, please, remember my pen. You're my favorite.

Finally in November—six months later—I announced on a diary page:

> Joanne came up to me in class. She had my pen and gave it to me! Thank you, Saint Anthony. I knew you'd come through.

CHAPTER FOUR

EVE'S SHADOW

Sexuality was foreign and frightening to the innocent girl I was. Other than glimpses of naked bodies in publications like National Geographic, facts about sex and my own changing body were not discussed at home or at my parochial school. American society in the 1950s had a prudish element, and the patriarchal undertones in the Catholic Church, which I absorbed like a sponge, equated women's sexuality with sin and shame. As a female I was the descendant of Eve, the temptress fruit vendor.

The teachers who shaped my early knowledge were nuns, swathed like Bedouins in layers of black, only their faces and hands showing evidence of being human. Like my classmates, I thought they lacked full bodies. I never saw them eat and wondered if they went to the bathroom.

I had no models for normal female sexual behavior. When Dad reached for Mom to give her a squeeze or a passionate kiss in front of me, she would shyly push him away. I didn't get to see them in amorous moments—and the normalcy of puberty's arrival was anything but that for me. My mother had not told me about menstruation, but even knowing would not have spared me the shock.

Sunday the whole family was attending Mass. I was twelve, quietly sitting in the pew with my missal open. My entire abdomen suddenly clenched into a fist; my insides seized up. The frightening pain came and stayed. Feeling faint, I whispered to my mother that I was sick. We were sitting toward the front of the church, and my face burned with embarrassment when she and my older brother each grabbed one of my arms to hurry down the center aisle to the exit. I knew everyone in church was staring at me.

I don't know if my mother suspected what was happening, but once home, and grounded in her belief that a bowel movement was a cure for any malady, she helped me upstairs.

In the bathroom, the grinding pain increased and I felt something wet between my legs. Blood was running down them. Mom told me to stand in the tub. Now fist-sized clots were falling from my body. "Mommy, what's happening to me?" I screamed. "Why am I bleeding?" There was so much blood. "Am I going to die?"

"Shush, Rie, it's going to be okay. Don't cry. You're just having your first period." While her tone suggested this was normal, perhaps even she wondered if it was.

Standing there in the bloody bathtub, I felt deeply wounded. My introduction into puberty, into womanhood, was a frightening ordeal. When I later saw my father after the scene in the bathroom, something was lost; I was no longer his innocent little girl. Somehow I had betrayed him.

Lack of a healthy attitude about sex is obvious in my early teen diary entries, where I wrote of "longing to be seven again so I wouldn't have to worry about sex and boys."

One day my friends and I were playing together, and we took a quiz on innocence. We all giggled a lot, but I felt awkward. Later that night I wrote:

> *... it was all about bedrooms and petting and that sort of disgusting stuff. The test showed I was the most innocent. I felt I should be proud of that fact ... but it ruined my day.*

Not long after that I was watching a TV show about two kids who had to get married. It was about making babies, and my mother said it was trash and not to watch it, but after that part was over, I did watch the rest.

In spite of my difficult transition into puberty, the rigid mores of Catholicism, and my responsibilities at home, my classmates considered me one of the popular girls in my co-ed grade school. I was invited to all the parties where Spin the Bottle was the highlight. While many of my peers possessed more male-female savvy by eighth grade than I did, my heart began to flutter if Joey's spin pointed my way and I got a shy peck on the cheek.

When I advanced to dating and proms my parents and younger siblings waited with me in the living room for my beau to arrive. In the fifties, formal dresses were like nineteenth-century ball gowns, with circular hoops to puff out the skirt. One evening, my boyfriend, Michael, was taking me to his prom. When he entered our house, it was so quiet; only my parents were there with me. He asked where the usual gang of gawkers were. Imagine his shock when my four younger siblings, huddled under my hooped skirt, jumped out to surprise him. Michael stood there nonplussed while we all had a good laugh.

At fifteen I worked after school and weekends at Lit Brothers Department Store, where I collected a new circle of friends, especially boys from other parts of the city. They were different, more mature than my high school peers, perhaps because they had jobs and adult responsibilities. They drove me home from work and invited me to the movies.

Throughout my high school years at Holy Child Academy my closet was full of thrift-store prom dresses, and names like Jack, Joe, and Jimmy were scribbled on my weekend calendar. But when an evening date was winding down in the car or on the front porch, each guy bumped into my wall. The feel of a boy's arm around me or holding hands in the theater was delicious, but I shut down when he became amorous. While I was still a high school sophomore, a college boy wanted to kiss me after the first two dates, but I pulled back protesting, "No, I'm saving myself for marriage." The truth was that his mature virility and obvious desire frightened me. I only wanted sweetness—not sex.

Fear of male sexuality held my libido a blindfolded hostage.

In the high school yearbook the list of my involvements under my senior photo revealed my many activities.

Yet for all my popularity and accomplishments, an invisible difference existed between my peers and me—a deep yearning for something other than the pull of males, marriage, and babies consuming my girlfriends. My sexuality was buried under religious restrictions, and marriage seemed mundane. Having helped raise five younger brothers and sisters, responsibility for more children wasn't appealing. I believed something deeper and more meaningful was calling my name.

ANNAMARIE BERNADETTE McCULLION

1205 Larchmont Ave.
Havertown, Pa.

Representative of Class 2,3,4; Cheerleader 2; Art Club 2; Mission Club 1; Althean 2,3,4; Mary Notes 4; Honor Roll 1,2,3,4; National Honor Society 4 Dramatic Club 3,4.

A seemingly minor incident in my teens also negatively influenced my feelings toward men.

One Saturday night I arrived home from my sales job. Through a doorway in the entrance foyer, I saw my parents sitting at the kitchen table, Mom's head bent like a reprimanded child while Dad scolded her for spending too much money. I understood his worry about finances—he had to support a large family on a small salary, but I felt he was wrong to chastise her. Mom was frugal and only bought the necessities for a household of kids. It upset me that he was treating her like an inferior.

That painful image of my mother being shamed was like a hot brand pressed into my mind. In that moment, an unspoken vow burrowed into my young psyche: I would never bow my head before any man.

CHAPTER FIVE

THE CALL

By senior year of high school thoughts of becoming a foreign missionary took on urgency as questions about my plans became the focus of most conversations with relatives and friends.

"What are you going to do after you finish school?"

"Have you applied for a job yet?"

"Are you seriously dating anybody?"

College was not an option for many of the girls in my neighborhood; they would become secretaries, nurses, or wives. Those choices seemed too ordinary for me; I believed myself destined for greater things.

During that last school year—1960—I researched Catholic communities of religious women, searching for an organization that would fulfill my vision of international medical service. The Peace Corps was not yet established, so the only option—from my limited perspective—was religious life.

There are three categories of religious women: the contemplatives who dedicate their lives to cloistered prayer; the teaching and nursing sisters who work mostly in the United States; and the missionaries who serve in foreign countries. Only the last group grabbed my interest. To me, they were the Marine Corps in the world of nuns. My sole desire was to provide hands-on medical care in those underprivileged countries so vivid in my imagined world.

As I wrote in my diary:

> *I don't want to preach to a dying person lying on a dirty street in India that God loves them; I want to heal them and make them better, so they can live more fully.*

This single concern was driven by a precocious understanding that caring for the sick and dying—tangible compassion—was a more meaningful Christian act than trying to convert native peoples to my religion.

I was drawn to Medical Mission Sisters (MMS) after one interview at their motherhouse, where I learned they were the only religious community doing solely medical work. I wrote them asking to be considered for admission.

MEDICAL MISSION SISTERS
SOCIETY OF CATHOLIC MEDICAL MISSIONARIES, INC.

8400 PINE ROAD, FOX CHASE
PHILADELPHIA 11, PA., PIlgrim 2-6100

August 22, 1960

Miss Annamarie McCullion
1205 Larchmont Avenue
Havertown, Pennsylvania

Dear Miss McCullion,

After reviewing your application for admission to our Society, I am happy to be able to tell you that you have been accepted for the next group of postulants that is to enter in October, 1960.

Soon you will be hearing from the Mistress of Postulants, who will send you the list of clothing and other articles which you will need, and other necessary information. We will inform you of the exact date of entrance as soon as it is set.

May God bless you and Our Lady keep you under her protection in your resolve to dedicate your life as a Medical Missionary.

Sincerely in Christ,

Mother M. Benedict

Mother M. Benedict, S.C.M.M.,M.D.
Provincial

Their letter arrived on August 25, 1960. Unable to face what was inside the envelope, I asked my mother to read it to me. The community accepted me as a candidate for that October. Later that night I confessed to my diary the anxiety the letter triggered. It confronted me with the reality that I would soon be leaving my family and friends. My life turned that day from the realm of the possible to the inevitable. Having endowed the decision from MMS with the power of God's will, I was committed. I wrote in my diary, "There's no turning back. It's done."

I was never pressured to join the convent. Neither the parish priests, the nuns at school, nor my own family encouraged me to make that choice. Mom and Dad would have preferred I stay near home, but like good Catholic parents they accepted my decision to respond to a "higher life." My parents never advised me what to do as I was growing up, though I sometimes wished they would, but they apparently felt I was capable of making good decisions on my own.

My understanding was that I was being invited—even required—to say yes to the inner nudging I believed was God's voice. Everything I had experienced up to that time in my small world, as well as my sense of the larger world, drew me to that choice.

As I imagined it at that young age, a calling to religious life meant I would have to do what I was told by superiors, cease having my own things, and abstain from sex. The price didn't seem too high for the seventeen-year-old I was. I was accustomed to obeying, and in a family of eight kids, I didn't have much that was just mine. We often wore used clothes that my mother's aunt brought us, and it always felt like Christmas when she came to visit my family.   And chastity—all I knew was that sex produced babies, and I wasn't interested in having children. It was too much work from what I saw in my family, and I had no understanding of the joy of sexual pleasure and of giving life to a child.

In early September I wrote about a farewell party my friends threw for me:

> Today, my friends came to say good-bye. Everyone was there: my old eighth-grade gang, girls from high school, and some kids I didn't even know. I cried so many times when I had to say good-bye to all of them, especially Jimmy. Some of my other boyfriends didn't even know of my plans to become a nun. I hadn't told them until now. I was afraid they'd think I was weird.

At the same time I also felt quite heroic telling everyone I was leaving home to become a medical missionary in distant lands.

After that night's journal entry I tucked the locked diaries of my last four years into a small box and pushed it into the back of my closet. It was like putting away the things of a child. My thoughts and concerns now shifted to a serious focus over the next months—preparation to become a Medical Mission Sister. Not yet eighteen, I hovered on the brink of leaving home and beginning an unknown journey into a new existence.

Last night home — October 10, 1960.

CHAPTER SIX

TIME TO SAY GOOD-BYE

The Society of Catholic Medical Missionaries, better known as Medical Mission Sisters or MMS, was founded in 1925 by Anna Dengel, an Austrian physician. Working in pre-partition India in the early 1920s, she witnessed the plight of Muslim women in *purdah*, the custom of being veiled and separated from men. The women couldn't receive direct medical care from male doctors, and they had no access to female physicians. Their dire need mobilized Anna to action. Far ahead of her times and possessing courage and an unstoppable vision, she traveled to the United States to gather a small group of medically-trained Western women to bring health care to their Muslim sisters. The first four women became a Catholic religious community and grew to serve in eighteen countries, establishing hospitals, rural clinics, and medical training facilities for indigenous people.

That woman, Anna, with the same name as my mom, was to become my spiritual mother—a woman I would meet several times in the years ahead. I was honored to know her, to be known by her.

I left home on October 11, 1960, to begin my twelve-year odyssey as a Medical Mission Sister. Jesus challenged his listeners to "leave father and mother, brothers and sisters, and even one's own life" to be his follower.

I heard the challenge and said, "Yes, I will do this."

The motherhouse in Philadelphia served as the American headquarters for the preparation of young women wanting to engage in the international work of healing. At the time I joined there were approximately seven hundred members serving around the world.

Several years of formation—akin to military boot camp—were required to prepare for both religious life and medical mission work. It was physically, spiritually, and emotionally rigorous—with no weekend passes—a "24/7" life.

The day I left home to enter MMS I asked my family to wait while I ran upstairs. Our neighbor had just put my two-year-old brother, Michael, down for a nap. My parents felt it best not to bring him. I couldn't leave before giving him one last good-bye kiss. I grieved that he would not remember me—that I wouldn't get to watch him grow through the toddler years or his childhood, as I did with my other younger siblings. Choking back sobs, I tucked the blanket around his soft baby shoulders. It was a last gesture of my love for him before rushing out to the waiting car.

*

The hour-long drive that October day from my home in the southwest suburbs of Philly to the motherhouse on the opposite side of the city was agony. My parents, siblings, and I were like wooden block people, squeezed beside each other in silence as the dreaded separation approached with each passing mile. Anticipation and anxiety scuffled in me, that strange mix of emotions that surface during significant events.

Guilt edged my thoughts. I was abandoning my family, especially my mother, for I had been her right hand. *How could I leave them? Yet, how could I deny this call from God?*

Caught up in my own feelings, I wasn't able to consider what my parents were enduring. The demands of my chosen life would require that they sacrifice free access to me forever.

In the 1959 movie *The Nun's Story,* the day Sister Luke enters a Belgian religious community shows the wrenching separation of a daughter from her parent when the closing bell rings for her to enter the cloister. In her last exchange with her father, she promised to do her best, but he pleaded that he only wanted her to be happy. As all the young candidates filed into the convent's inner sanctum, they stole poignant glances back at their families, tears welling in their eyes.

That scene was recreated for me as I gathered with the other new candidates and their families in a large hall on the Medical Mission Sisters' property. Tension charged the room, bouncing off the tight faces and surfacing in strained conversations.

Shortly into the visit, the other candidates and I were called away to change into gray, ankle-length dresses with demure Peter Pan collars. Our return thirty minutes later confronted our families with evidence that we were already changing from daughter and sister to a different, less recognizable person—a fledgling nun, called a postulant.

Me as a postulant.

My first letter home, written five days later, described my new life:

My dearest family,

I suppose you are waiting with bated breath to hear about convent life, so I'll keep you in suspense no longer—I love it! The girls and sisters are just great, my days are full, the physical work is extremely hard, and, oh—the food is delicious!

When the bell signaled the time for families to leave the other day, I wanted to cling to Dad and escape with you all, run after your departing tail lights.

I was bereft after you left, but then the sister-in-charge led me downstairs to meet the other twenty-four postulants from all over the US and Canada, and I was pleasantly distracted by meeting these girls. We will be a new group of forty when the last contingent arrives.

That evening, we walked up from our building to the main chapel to pray the rosary and eat supper. We sit at tables of six in a large dining hall at the main building, and after our first few days of talking during meals, we now speak only at the midday dinner. During the other two meals, a sister reads over a microphone from a spiritual book. After the silent evening meal, we have an hour of recreation and then end the day with prayer in our smaller chapel.

We are in bed by 9:00 p.m. I love the nightly shower after growing up with only a bathtub, but the water is usually cold, so I don't stay under it for long!

Each dorm sleeps six. I have a narrow bed, a wooden chair, a built-in closet with space for hanging my two gray dresses, one drawer, and three shelves. A long green curtain, like they have in hospitals, runs along a track in the ceiling to draw around our little cubicles when we are dressing.

The next morning, a sister came at 5:40 a.m., called out some Latin phrase that I didn't understand, and we were supposed to respond "Deo Gratis," which means "Thanks be to God." I didn't feel very thankful at that hour of the morning—it was still dark!

Pulling myself together, I joined the others in the cold walk over to the main chapel for Mass and a silent breakfast. Later we had an orientation class, then worked for several hours carrying heavy wooden desks up several flights of stairs for the new library.

After the midday meal we tramped around the farm, chatting and munching on apples from the trees here, peeked into the barns, and walked down the gravel road to the MMS cemetery. In the afternoon, more classes, more work, more eating and evening recreation. The day is punctuated by prayer times. The kneelers in the chapel are wood with no padding, so my knees are seriously hurting, but everyone says calluses will form and they won't pain so much.

One evening this past week we had a weenie-roast outside and sat around the fire roasting marshmallows. Someone started the song, "When Irish Eyes are Smiling" and I burst into tears. Most days I've been so busy I don't have time to feel homesick—but then something like that song catches me and that deep-belly missing starts. Getting lonely and homesick is a part of this life I have chosen, but I hope, Mom and Dad, you aren't sad because of my decision.

I am happy here, and I want you all to be happy and not worry about me. At night, when I am alone in the quiet of my little cubicle, I look out my window toward the southeast and wonder what you are all doing at home.

Well, a bell just rang, so I must go.

Love, Rie

P.S. My eyebrows are growing in, and I'm gaining weight. Oh dear, what will I look like when you and the rest of my family and friends see me at our first visiting day in three months?

CHAPTER SEVEN

SILENCE AND PRAYER

The centuries-old tradition of silence in religious communities was intended to foster an inner space to allow an awareness of God's intimate presence. Even though I came from a large and noisy family and was quite talkative, I found the practice of silence surprisingly easy. The only times I experienced quiet growing up was when I hid myself in my room with a book or attended early weekday Mass.

During those first three years of formation, we maintained silence except for our midday meal and two hours of recreation, afternoon and evening, when we played board games, listened to music, went for walks, or just talked with each other.

We spoke in class, of course, and when work or study required it, but in whispers so as not to disturb others. One morning after breakfast my superior motioned me from the main hallway into a coat closet to tell me that I stirred my morning coffee too loudly.

In the midst of listening in serious silence to a book being read aloud at mealtimes, it was not uncommon for the young postulants or novices to find something to giggle at. My group seemed especially prone to losing our silence in our first months there. One incident was my fault. A huge bowl of homegrown salad was placed in the center of the table, right in front of where I sat . . . and I spied two long antennae waving at me over the rim of the bowl. I giggled—and soon everyone at my table was laughing.

For several weeks I was assigned to read aloud for the noon meals. One day I caused the entire room to break the silence when I misspoke. In lieu of reading, "His Holiness," I said over the microphone, "Upon the election of his Holy-nose, Pope John the XXIII . . . " Even the superiors lost control and laughed.

I came to value the quiet, which allowed a satisfying concentration on a task, but I found my solitude more self-centered than God-centered. Aware that I was continually being assessed for my suitability for that life, I became increasingly introspective, comparing myself to the other sisters, who all seemed holier, more intelligent, and more talented than I.

Silence can nurture spiritual development or feed runaway self-analysis; I struggled with the latter tendency, feeling inadequate for the vocation I thought God had called me to, often doubting if I was going to be acceptable to that community of women.

Only once can I remember the rule of silence as painful. During my first novitiate year, one of my favorite sister novices had been losing weight, her habit hanging loosely from her bony shoulders. One afternoon while crossing from one room to another, I glanced down the hall and saw her standing in the filtered shafts of sun in the entryway. She stared silently at me for a long time. Then, with a subtle movement of her right hand, she waved to me. She was missing from supper that night. I felt devastated by her departure. That custom of secret departures felt unfair to those who left and to all of us who remained. We had no chance to say good-bye.

*

Silence and prayer formed the platform of religious life. My understanding of prayer had to expand beyond my childhood missal and memorized prayers. It proved to be one of my hardest challenges.

Each morning and night we prayed the Church's Divine Office—traditional scripture readings and prayers aligned with certain hours. There was also daily meditation, Mass, the rosary, Gregorian Chant, and our own private prayer times. As an aspiring nun kneeling in chapel, my hands clasped on the pew's edge and my head bent, I would peek at the faces of the older sisters with their eyes closed and lips silently moving and wonder what they were praying about.

My short life was a shallow reservoir to draw from. I was a beggar digging through cans in search of some pious devotion. I had my rote petitions to God: *Please take care of my family. Bless the work of our sisters in all our missions. Give peace to the world.* Then running out of intentions, my thoughts usually turned to how much my knees hurt on the hard wooden kneelers.

After rising at five each morning and praying the Office, we were expected to meditate. I didn't know about "morning and night people" in those days, but I have since learned that I am a true night person. That half hour of sitting motionless in a warm, quiet chapel before sunrise was my Waterloo.

February 1961 letter home:

> We have meditation every day from 5:30 to 6:00 a.m. in the chapel, and it seems I have been sleeping through it. At the dinner table today my superior asked: "Who is the one in the second row during meditation, who's bent so far over I can't see her from the back of chapel?" I was sitting at her table that day and had to admit that, possibly, it was me. (I think she knew.) It's not good to be sleeping during meditation. In the first weeks here, I used to think, "What if I want to leave?" But now I worry, "What if they ask me to go?"

March 1961 letter home:

> In my last letter, I mentioned how badly I was doing at meditation. Well, for the past few weeks, I've been in the back pew—kneeling, while everyone else sits, to help me stay awake. I still doze a bit, but not for long since I tend to slip from the kneeler when I drift off.

My parents probably had no idea of what meditation entailed, but were surely sympathetic as to how hard it was for me to stay awake.

My difficulty with meditation persisted even after I became a novice. In a July letter home, I confessed:

> Early morning meditation is still such a problem for me. My superior gave me a cup and a small jar of coffee to drink in my cubicle when I first wake up. However, it's instant coffee with no milk or sugar, and I could only get hot tap water from the bathroom. Besides tasting like poison, it didn't keep me awake.

That idea failing, my superior had me stand in the back of the chapel during the half hour of meditation, but a few backward glances from her pew revealed a young novice leaning against the back wall—asleep.

The last recourse was to have me sit next to her. That scared me into alertness, but after a few successful days staying awake out of fear, I woke up one morning with my head on her shoulder and a resigned grimace on her face. I thought, "I may be incorrigible. Can I still become a Medical Mission Sister if I can't stay awake for meditation?"

All the proceeds from the sale of this book,
Of Human Clay
are used to install wells and latrines
in Malawi, Africa,
one of the most impoverished countries in the world.

The **Vision** of Fresh Water Project International, a small
501c organization with an on-site Malawian Director is:

**Every Malawian has access
to clean water and sanitation.**

For more information, go to:

freshwaterintl.org

CHAPTER EIGHT

WORK AND PLAYS

Hard physical labor was another dimension of preparation for the rigors of mission work ahead. Tropical climates, the ruggedness of travel in undeveloped countries, and limited resources created a physically demanding environment for our sisters.

As postulants we were expected to help maintain the property and demonstrate our physical endurance. I loved the challenge and felt up to whatever I was asked to do. Each month we circulated through various tasks. My first job was scrubbing the stairwell steps in our building: six flights—seventy-six steps—four landings. The surface of each step was covered in tiny ceramic tiles that dug indentations in my knees. I felt like a charwoman.

Then I moved on to the damp kitchen basement, where I peeled hundreds—no, thousands—of vegetables for our community meals for several weeks. My hands were covered with nicks and cuts from the knife blades.

In subsequent letters home I informed my family of further assignments:

I have a new job—the sewing room. I broke two sewing machine needles and jammed the machine in the first three days. The sister in charge switched me to hand sewing.

My next month's assignment:

Now I'm slaving away in the laundry these days. Its hot and steamy and I sweat a lot in my habit, big trickles of wetness running down inside all these layers of clothing. It feels gross.

A month later I recounted another work responsibility:

I had a big thrill on Saturday. One of the postulants whose job was working on the farm got a bad case of poison ivy. (That's not the big thrill.) I had to take her place and drive the tractor. It was so much fun! But the worst part of the farm assignment required catching and decapitating squawking chickens for dinner. They made me so nervous with their clucking and flapping around—even after their heads were cut off!

The food we ate was mostly homegrown, and I picked beets, carrots, and corn on the farm. Eggs from our chickens and milk from our cows gave us the freshest of ingredients, and the homemade bread tasted delicious. It was no wonder my waist thickened.

The most challenging assignment I had in those first years was being the regulator—the sister responsible for getting up earlier than everyone else to ring the wake-up bell. I had to get up at 4:50 a.m. I wrote my family with my worries about that job: "How will I survive? What if I don't hear the bedside alarm and oversleep?" The regulator was key to the timely day's start of our structured routines. No lateness in that ordered life.

Once woken, we quickly dressed in the dark, did our morning toilette, and flowed like silent lava down the staircase and into our small chapel for an hour, followed by a five-minute walk to the main chapel where we attended Mass. Then breakfast *finally* came. After another visit to the chapel for individual prayer, we did our work assignments, attended classes, and returned for a noontime meal, where we could speak while we ate.

Talking was allowed for another hour afterwards, when we were free to do whatever we wanted. We usually played sports, went on walks, listened to or played music, darned our stockings, and wrote or read letters. On the infrequent days we received mail, I'd tuck myself in a corner, away from the group, to savor the treasured letters from home.

The afternoon was spent in more work and classes or study time, which carried us to the silent supper meal and another free hour of recreation. Our superior would ring a bell that ended the hour's free time and signaled Grand Silence, a period that began at eight p.m. with the antiphonal evening prayers in chapel and continued until after Mass the next morning. Grand Silence meant that you could not speak or look at anyone unless your life depended on it.

After bedtime preparations, a nine p.m. bell meant we had to be *in* bed. Several times I had to make a dive for my mattress or try to lean precariously on my wooden chair to reach something in my closet after the bell had rung—I couldn't put my feet back on the floor. If I did, I had to report it to my superior and would be given some form of penance to do, like washing windows.

Yet all was not work, prayer, and study. We also had parties on holidays and holy days and produced plays for special occasions. I loved drama and acting from high school. During my three years in formation I did a soft-shoe dance to "April Showers," acted as a gangster in an 1890s skit, and was the lead character, Emily, in *Our Hearts Were Young and Gay.* I also directed a Broadway-quality performance of *Antigone.*

It was a creative time for me. With another sister I adapted a stage play from a book and acted the part of the tough, cigar-smoking salesman. I also wrote an original script called *The Journey,* which was performed twice for the entire community of sisters, who were amazed when I was introduced as the playwright. Surrounded by loud applause, I almost fainted with pride.

*

Life as a young nun at the motherhouse was rich with other activities besides prayer and work.

Besides the arts, we were quite athletic: hiking in the surrounding park-lands, skating on a nearby pond in winter, and playing sports. I wrote home about how seriously we took winning:

> People may think we go around praying all day,
> but we don't. I want to tell you about our injuries.
> Almost everyday, weather allowing, we play baseball,
> volleyball, or basketball, and all ladylike behavior
> disappears on the court. We've had one black eye, two
> sprained ankles, three pairs of broken glasses, one
> candidate knocked unconscious, one cracked head,
> and random cuts and scrapes. Until last Thursday I
> remained unharmed, but in the last five minutes of
> a basketball game, I hit the ground three times, taking
> someone down with me with each fall. I bruised my
> elbow and knee and ripped a huge tear in my stocking.
> It's the sixth hole I've had to darn. After the third fall I
> was pulled from the game. The sister referee said I was a
> threat to the team's safety.

My experiences were not what most people imagine life in a convent to be. Each day found me living and learning among strong women striving to live holy lives and serve the poor and sick in foreign lands. A growing love for those I called "my sisters" took root in me.

Already, several of my group had left, either by their choice or being asked to leave. I only hoped I could stick it out and be accepted into the next phase—the novitiate—after those ten months as a postulant.

CHAPTER NINE

RISING EXPECTATIONS

My postulancy progressed through 1961. I was expected to absorb more of the behaviors appropriate for an aspiring Medical Mission Sister.

I lived with women from all over the US and several other nations. Most of the professed (vowed) members had served in one or more of the many countries where we had missions. As a parochial girl with no real travel experience, I breathed in the rich air stirred up by interaction with these global citizens.

The medical orientation of their services and the professional education of the sisters balanced scientific study and the work of compassionate healing. As one of the newer religious communities, MMS didn't fit the stereotypical image of the cloistered nun or the teacher with the raised wooden ruler. They were more "roll up your sleeves and get to work" women. That all rubbed off on me while setting a high bar for a fresh eighteen-year-old.

The first three years of preparation—ten months as a postulant and two years as a novice—focused on molding and toughening us. In January 1961, a few months into the process, I wrote to my parents that things would be changing when I became a novice later that year. No longer allowed to receive letters from boys, I asked my parents to tell Johnny, Gary, and Zaf that I was sorry, but they couldn't write to me anymore.

In spite of those constraints on my social life, my face breaking out in pimples, my eyebrows growing in like my father's, and missing my family—I was happy.

The changes in me were not only external. Classes in Christian doctrine, scripture, and mission history deepened my awareness of the intense expectations that came with being a Medical Mission Sister. At eighteen I was also moving from adolescence into young womanhood with all the self-absorption inherent in that transition.

In February, I wrote in my journal:

> Life is so challenging and confusing—and I am just beginning to realize it. I thought I knew me, but I am discovering otherwise. I am quite different from what I thought—much more serious—though I still joke a lot. I used to think I was a funny person with a serious side. Now I think I am a serious person with a funny side— but I don't really know.

My father had told me before I joined MMS that my new life would bring me peace, but I came to realize that peace did not come with any one way of life, but only from the hard struggle to find it. I was trying to do just that—find peace.

In a July 1961 letter home to my parents, I had to tell them of the new rules that were coming:

> I am sorry to break the news of the new novitiate rules regarding visiting and letter writing. We can only exchange one letter a month and there are only four visiting days per year with immediate family and only ONE all year for relatives and friends. It's about learning detachment from what we are attached to— and you, my family, are my biggest attachment. The second novitiate year will be more lenient, but this first year is considered the time of real testing of our vocations.

I didn't give much thought to the painful separation that my life choice required of my parents, although my dad, with a wink, found ways to circumvent the rules. He often showed up at the motherhouse with gifts or donations for our medical mission work—and hoping to catch a peek at his beloved oldest daughter.

Toward the end of my ten months as a postulant I wrote to the sector superior of our American community, who had just returned from India, "I humbly ask permission to be received into the novitiate and to wear the habit of the Society of Catholic Medical Missionaries." If accepted, I would begin to wear the habit: a gray dress with an overlaid panel and a white veil. That novice outfit, like any uniform, set me apart, declared that I was different.

I also submitted three requests for a new religious name to signify that I was a changed person: Sister Ann Thomas, to honor my beloved parents; Sister Aimee; or Sister Simeon, but I might not have gotten any of my choices and instead have been given

Photo of me as a novice that my father carried in his wallet.

Sister Somnolence for sleeping during meditation.

The day of entering the novitiate began with a simple ceremony in which my postulant group entered the chapel accompanied by the choir singing. At the altar we each received a folded white cotton veil and a strand of large rosary beads. Then we walked out and returned wearing the white veil and headdress, with the rosary beads hanging from snaps on the left side of our habit. As we knelt at the altar rail, our sector superior announced our religious names one by one. After the final blessing by the officiating priest, we processed down the aisle to the outside where our families were waiting. I now looked like a nun, though several days passed before I managed to keep my peaked headdress centered.

In a letter sent home after that ceremony I wrote of some of the tensions tugging at me:

> Hello from a seven-day-old novice. Others have to call me about four times before I realize that Sister Aimee and me are the same person.
>
> I'm sorry that I cried when everyone was leaving. The thought that I won't be seeing many family and friends for a whole year was so painful.
>
> Can you understand how it feels to immerse myself in this life and try to dim the lights of past relationships, only to be right in the middle of everyone again?
>
> I wanted to show that the convent hasn't changed me, but it has. I can see how different I have become in my attitudes and behaviors. I used to yearn for my past life at home, or wondered what else I could be if I weren't here, but now after our three-day retreat and this visiting day, I can see that the outside secular and materialistic world I left has no great interest for me. I want to live a life fully dedicated to loving service in the footsteps of Jesus. This is the only way for me. All I want in life can be found here.
>
> Sister Aimee

How hard it must have been for my parents to read that last sentence. Yet I had sensed, even as a young girl, that I wanted more than what I saw in the culture around me.

That was the first letter I signed as Sister Aimee, instead of all my earlier letters, which had ended with "Love, Rie."

My novitiate years were an increasingly challenging time, as was intended. The demands and expectations grew as the superior worked to shape us still worldly young women. The daily silence became heavier and the penances for slips in behavior more frequent. My self-induced pressure to be perfect intensified.

December 1961 letter home:

> It would be silly to try to pretend I'm not homesick during this season. All the happy memories of past Christmases arrive with December. I feel your absence especially on these cold, clear-sky nights walking back from supper in the dark when all the neighboring houses look so warm with their Christmas lights and trees sparkling in windows. This life isn't lonely by any means, but there are many times when I am drawn into a place of deep aloneness. Though there may be touches of melancholy, God's love and the magnetism of our mission work strengthens me against my own selfish desires. Oh, there is so much to learn and so much to do, yet so little time—just one small life—and it must be done well.

In February 1962 only immediate family were allowed to visit. In a subsequent letter I tried to comfort my parents as we all struggled with the long separations:

> I'm afraid our visiting day came in the middle of a difficult period and you probably went away worried. You never need to be concerned about me, even though I may talk like the sky is falling. When I entered, I did so because I felt God called me to do this. I was not primarily focused on becoming "a nun"—it just seemed the only way I knew to do medical work in poor countries. I would never think of leaving unless my superiors decided I did not have a true calling to this life.

The upset you witnessed came from my fear that I'm not capable of fitting into this community, even though Saint Paul said, "God has chosen the weak things of this world." But after talking with my superior of novices, I believe and hope that my weakness will not be wiped away, but used as God wants.

Insecurity and loneliness occasionally showed up during those years in formation despite living in a large community of women. But sexuality was never an issue for me in the convent. We spent our days within one square mile of the motherhouse property, leaving mainly for a doctor or dentist appointment. The only males we saw regularly were tottering Father Maloney, our aging chaplain, and his male dog Harry. Occasionally visiting bishops or priests would come, but we young nuns only saw their backs at the front of chapel saying Mass.

In our religious life class, we were counseled to avoid "particular friend-ships," a veiled reference to homosexuality, a concern in same-sex communities. That admonishment went right over my head. I had no idea of that reality until a few years later, when I learned that my younger brother Johnny, who later died from AIDS, was gay.

I thought particular friendships meant showing favorites, which could be destructive of a sense of community. I struggled with feeling natu-rally drawn to some sisters more than others, though over time an easy comraderie developed with all my peers.

The girls in my entrance group were from diverse backgrounds and I liked them all except for one who seemed odd—very intense and nervous. At recreation one day, she had been knitting in a corner. We invited her to join our small circle standing around chatting. She had two knitting needles in one hand and repeatedly pushed the long plastic needles up and down onto her other hand. I didn't realize how intense the motion was until I saw she had driven them through her palm! Blood dripped onto the floor. We stared open-mouthed at her hand, with the ends of the needles protruding out the other side.

She wasn't at supper that night . . . or ever after.

But the others were engaging and fun companions: a Canadian, who had a twisted neck but could play a mean jazz piano; carrot-haired Stella, who looked just like Little Orphan Annie; and Maria, who emigrated from Italy when she was fourteen and still had a strong accent. One candidate came from a wealthy family, and another was a peanut of a girl from a poor town in Texas who walked in her sleep. Several of the candidates were older and had gone to college or nursing school. Carol had been in the army. Some were quiet and gentle like Angela, who was part Native American, part Mexican, while others were lively like Regina, who always played the clown.

We were different sizes and shapes, from many states, Canada, and the Philippines, and our various accents prompted mutual teasing. It was an ordinary mixture of young women who could have been plucked from anywhere, but for the unique calling we all believed we had heard in our hearts.

In our academic courses a brilliant faculty of sisters taught concepts that challenged my understanding of life. I often questioned if I was smart enough. My mind and old beliefs were being stretched by the new ideas covered in my studies: comparative religion, linguistics, and cultural anthropology, among others.

Who was I and how did I fit into this new existence, which went far beyond my early expectations?

In a September 1962 letter to my parents, I wrote:

> I can remember how I told you without qualms in my first weeks here that I might be in the missions for the rest of my life. I thought it was all rather adventurous until the other night when I saw our promotional movie, "A Different Story." Watching the departure scene of sisters in their white habits bound for the foreign missions, I realized that the novitiate days are

brief, and that the life which lies ahead is going to demand everything from me. I am grateful that these insights have come now, as they enable me to truly value this last year here in the quiet of the novitiate and to accept with joy the difficult, yet meaningful, life ahead. Pray for me that I may be formed now as I should be. I have so much "becoming" still to do.

CHAPTER TEN

THE BUBBLE

W hile we novices were quite secluded from the events swirling outside our community and compound, we were kept informed of critical issues happening in those tumultuous sixties. The intent of that isolation was to allow us to detach from cultural trends and secular ways of thinking and acting in order to cultivate a new identity. Once we entered the active ministry, the social and political realities would become the environment in which we embedded our work. Being well informed was crucial for any Medical Mission Sister. However, during my formation years from 1960 until 1963, candidates and novices were just told of certain major events and only exposed to religious or cultural programs.

The Beatles were insects, as far as I knew.

But in November 1960 we were well aware of Kennedy's rise to the presidency. We were able to talk at supper because he won the election. A week before, the sister in charge of laundry had put big "Kennedy for President" buttons on each laundry basket delivered around our quarters, and discussions raged over the weeks leading up to election night.

And in a March 1962 journal I wrote:

> Last night Mr. Khan from the Pakistan embassy was
> invited to speak on Islam. How thought-provoking to
> meet someone who totally believes that his religion is
> as true as we Catholics believe ours is.

A few weeks later, a life-changing insight shook the complacency of my reaction to Mr. Kahn's talk. I was in our novitiate library, studying a chapter in my comparative religion textbook on Hinduism. It explained that the God Vishnu entered into a woman, Devaki, who gave birth to the man-god Krishna. Staring at the page, I felt as though my head exploded, blowing off my veil. That one sentence revealed the core of the course—all sacred texts are grounded in mythology, and all religions are temporal and cultural expressions of humankind's eternal search for meaning. Catholicism taught that it was the "one and only true religion," but I saw that no one belief system had ownership of truth. My unquestioning belief in that Church doctrine collapsed there in the library.

But rather than experiencing that as an abandonment of my faith, I felt liberated. I was born and raised in the Catholic Church, so it was a reasonable environment in which to explore my search for meaning. Mr. Kahn, born in Pakistan, sought the meaning of life through Islam. I wished I could have told him that evening, "Mr. Kahn, we are both right."

In my letters home, I often presumed to counsel my parents. When I read those letters now, I'm deeply embarrassed. I advised them to go on retreats and to read spiritual books, totally insensitive to the demands of their life with five children still at home, which didn't allow the luxuries that were available to me in my chosen life. And what did I think I knew—not yet twenty years old—against their maturity and wisdom? Yet once I became a nun, I thought it required me to assume some mantle of authority, as evident in an earnest letter to them in October 1962:

> I hope you are taking the threat of war very seriously, teaching the kids what to do in case of a missile attack. You might think of setting up the basement for a shelter. Here, we have been preparing with drills and plans for safety should anything happen with this Cuban missile crisis.

When I later became a professed sister, I had direct access to TV, newspapers, and magazines, rather than the secondhand reports through my superiors. In November 1963 I gathered with my sisters around our one TV, trying to grasp what had happened and its significance for our country. I commiserated with my parents in a letter about the shock and gruesome truth of Kennedy's murder. "I think that we ordinary citizens are oblivious to the tangled webs that lie behind what we see and hear on the news. What is it we aren't told?"

Again in March 1964 I preached my opinions on the political scene to my family:

> The Vietnamese people are suffering so, and I think America will soon discover that she has done a grave injustice. God forgive us for all the wrong we've done in our foreign relations... and what of all our young men dying for an uncertain—if not dishonorable— cause?

While I thought and prayed over the issues affecting my country and my world—the feminist movement, Martin Luther King Jr. and civil rights, and war protests—they had little impact on my daily routines during those first three years of training. I lived in a contained society, immersed in a process of socialization to a culture whose priorities were God, personal discipline, community needs, and service.

Perhaps because I was out of the media mainstream, my perspectives on national and world events questioned what was behind appearances and published information. I began to cultivate a healthy skepticism about politics to balance my innate idealism. Yet much of the cultural and political currents deeply embedded in the American psyche didn't flow through my life then; access to the news was limited during those years.

Conversations in later adulthood often left me feeling ignorant of both large and small events of the sixties, unable to contribute to the discussion or catch the jokes or references. I don't have the storehouse of stories from that turbulent decade that my peers possess, and I often find myself on the fringe of popular culture, even today.

CHAPTER ELEVEN

I MADE IT!

After passing through a three-year gauntlet of daily scrutiny to determine if I had the right stuff, I was invited to become a member of the Medical Mission Sisters community as a professed sister—one who takes the vows of poverty, chastity and obedience. Those binding promises have been the core of Catholic religious communities for centuries. The three vows required a life of deep sacrifice, for they sliced into our human desires for material possessions, physical pleasures, and independence. Their intent was to free us—to loosen us from our tight self-centeredness and enable us to readily respond to the needs of others. I had much to learn as I tried to plumb their depths and find out what those vows required of me in my day-to-day life.

The decision to make a permanent commitment was done in stages. If I continued, I would make initial vows for three years, renew them for two, and then make final vows—for life. At each renewal I was free to leave or could be asked to, as happened with many from my group over the years. Forty of us entered the starting gate in 1960; only twenty made first vows. Only twelve made it to final vows, myself included.

May 1963 letter home:

> My dear family,
>
> Fall on your knees and thank God. After three years of wondering and hoping, I and the nineteen other remaining second-year novices heard, "You have been accepted for profession."

*I don't think I can explain how I felt after that
announcement. How had I made it when others hadn't?*

August 1963 journal:

> *I've had several days of silent retreat before making
> my first vows tomorrow. During this time of reflection
> I came across a quote: "Flight is not good without
> a search." Had my choice of religious life been an
> escape from—or a reaching for—something? Critics of
> Catholic nuns suggest we fled to the convent out of fear
> of sex, or lacked an ego, or wanted to be taken care of.
> I've tried to measure myself against those charges.*

When I joined Medical Mission Sisters, perhaps I was fleeing from the
weight of too many responsibilities at home or the fear of being ordinary,
but was there more? Was I afraid of sex? Was I wanting security? Was I so
idealistic I couldn't adapt to American cultural norms?

And what was I searching for? Intimacy with God, status in my Catholic
community, the adventure of foreign countries, an opportunity to serve
those who had so little?

I suspect that both impulses—to run *from* and *to*—were inextricably
entwined, and all those strands of motives were so knotted together that
I still can't tease them apart, even after years of trying.

The ceremony of profession took place on August 15, 1963. I was so
nervous that morning, not only because of the profound significance of
the event, but also at the prospect of being on public display after three
relatively hidden years.

Organ music and choral harmonies provided a dramatic background as
I walked down the chapel aisle with the other novices. I blushed when I
saw the turned heads and emotion-filled eyes of my family and friends,
and calmed myself by staring at the floor. I wondered what my parents
were thinking as they saw their daughter about to lock in her life for

three more years. Were they happy? Proud? Sad? I hoped they could share in my joy at achieving that next step.

A solemn mood hung over the chapel, inviting the witnesses into hushed anticipation.

The bishop in his ritual garments waited at the front of the chapel to receive us. It was not unlike a marriage day, although I didn't think of it in "Bride of Christ" terms. The ceremony felt more like a graduation. The change in my status was signaled when I left the chapel in my white cotton novice veil and returned in the silky, azure-blue of a professed sister. Once back at the altar I knelt to have a chain with a silver crucifix lowered over my head. I pronounced my vows with a loud but quavering voice and received the bishop's blessing. Pride and awe splashed together inside me as I felt the weight of my act, but I knew this was what I wanted. I had no doubts.

The choir then burst into a joyful song to escort us newly professed sisters back down the aisle, ending the ceremony.

Outside, the mood was jubilant and hugs flew at me from every corner of the court-yard. I was overwhelmed by what I had just done, by the thrill of having my whole family there after a year of separation, and by being welcomed by professed sisters as one of them. I could see that my parents were proud of me—Dad stuck to my side, holding my hand, while Mom ushered family and friends up to me to say their congratulations.

I had made it.

Profession Day.

*

During my first year as a member, I was the community's "guest mistress," caring for the many visitors who came to our motherhouse. We often hosted bishops and priests from India, South America, and other nations who came to petition our community to bring our medical services to their people. I drove the guests to and from airports and to local sights and meetings. It was good they were unaware that I had just gotten my driver's license.

Preparation of meals and general assistance to our guests was another aspect of my work—and unfortunately, they *did* get to know I wasn't a good cook. But I was able to arrange for their laundry, provide them with phone numbers, or simply sit and visit with them during their solitary meals in the guest dining room.

In between those activities I handled the switchboard for the entire compound. I lost many a call in the early days before learning to avoid getting tangled in the cord while inserting the right metal plug into the correct blinking hole. With time, I even managed several incoming and outgoing calls at once.

This was the year when many of my entrance group with professional degrees received their mission assignments: Uganda, Venezuela, Vietnam. I often chauffeured those sisters to the airport to see them off. I wrote to my family in February 1964 of such a trip:

> On Saturday, I was told to drive one of the sisters in my group to the airport for her departure for India. Several others came with us. Saying good-bye to my friend of three years was hard—I probably won't see her again, unless I'm assigned to Delhi. After we cried our farewell, she left the airport waiting area. She looked so tiny, so alone, as she walked the fifty yards to the plane. When they pulled away the stairs and the plane turned around and rolled down the runway, the sense of letting go of a sister and friend left me in deep silence on the drive home.

My mostly happy life as an official MMS didn't relieve me of my recurring self-doubts and my continuous need to wrestle issues to the ground, as I did in a June 1964 journal entry:

> Living community life is truly a paradox. It is my deepest joy and my hardest trial. Just in the past few months I have had a difficult time figuring out how to deal with all the differences between other sisters and myself, and yet when I recently felt that all my supports were buckling under me, I became aware that God was still the buoyant object in my little puddle of self.
>
> Even the human support I receive from all of my family and sisters, while it greatly comforts me, does not set me fully at peace, because only God can give me that. As long as I can continue to love, that is what matters. I often fear that I will grow selfish in reaction to the heavy demands of God, and the religious and missionary life.

CHAPTER TWELVE

GOLD, POPES, AND POVERTY

How did we support ourselves, our work? I began to learn the answer as a newly professed sister when I was thrown into promotional and fundraising events along with my other assignments.

One sunny Sunday I accompanied a sister to a mother-daughter breakfast at a local girls' high school where she was the guest speaker. I was seated at the head table, and while Sister Jean was giving her talk, I happened to glance into the silver vase in front of me, saw my reflection, and marveled, *This is me, Rie, sitting here—but the audience thinks they are looking at a Medical Mission Sister.* I teared up. Since Sister was talking about Ghanaian children with leprosy, it appeared I was moved by her words, but I didn't hear her during that flash of insight about my changed identity.

On many weekends I joined small groups of available sisters who traveled to local parishes in Philadelphia to solicit funds, as well as to distant states like Illinois and Wisconsin. After the parish priest would speak about our medical missions during Mass, we would stand at the church doors to collect money from exiting parishioners. I always enjoyed that role; proud to be a Medical Mission Sister, proud to do what I could to raise money for our institutions around the world. When people looked away or passed me by, I felt a twinge of rejection, but most came up and dropped something in my basket or asked about our work.

Collecting money from people did make me more conscious of the vow of poverty. I thought about street beggars and the homeless and how it must feel for them. We depended on the generous donations of others not just for our missions, but also for the maintenance of our own lives.

Because of our dependence on the kindness of others and our vow of poverty, we lived from our needs, not our wants. Within our community we had to request toiletries, for instance, or another pair of stockings. We had to prove that we were walking on lumps from darning so many holes before we were issued a new pair of black cotton stockings.

One thing I was learning about that curious vow called poverty is that it wasn't about being destitute. I lived in a simple but comfortable environment, ate delicious homemade meals, had all the clothes I needed—four sets of habits: two for daily work, and a good one each for winter and summer—and two pairs of shoes. It was hard to feel the impact of this vow there on our compound when my basic needs were met. However, our commitment to the missions required leaving our own culture and living in one where unfamiliar customs, climates, and faces striped us of the known and comfortable.

In those early days of my training I tended to focus on the excitement of living in another country, yet I came to realize the emotional cost of our work. A sister who left for the missions wasn't able to come back to care for an aging parent, even if she was an only child. Those who learned that a family member was dying weren't able to return to say their last good-bye.

I was not only growing in awareness of the personal impact of that vow but was also becoming more distressed by the discrepancies I saw between the institutional church and what I was learning about the grinding poverty in "Third World" countries. The money it took to build and maintain the National Shrine of the Immaculate Conception disturbed me—its gold dome, stunning mosaics, and numerous chapels, as well as the cavernous main church, felt excessive. The extravagance seemed less about honoring the Blessed Mother and more about human ego. The use of the Catholic Church's wealth for buildings, rather than people, didn't make sense to me. I no longer felt my earlier awe at such structures but saw them as an abuse of the Church's true mission. Maybe "the poor are always with us" because we don't choose to create a more just and equitable society with our institutional wealth.

The pomposity of the services held at the Shrine—and the fine lace altar cloths, gold-trimmed vestments, and the jewelry the bishops and cardinals wore—were too much for me, too contrary to the message that Jesus brought.

My distress spilled over into a letter home in December 1963:

> I hope that the gift of Pope Paul's tiara to the poor
> is just the beginning of a long series of purges in the
> Church so that it will soon cease to be a museum of
> treasures and give of its wealth to the greater needs of
> humanity.

Such immense social injustice, poverty, and pain existed among our less fortunate brothers and sisters that it pained me to see my Church missing the point.

> Surely, we Christians must find our happiness
> bittersweet: grateful for what we are and have,
> yet feeling somewhat guilty when so many equally
> deserving people are denied even the necessities of life.

The idealism at the core of my personality generated tension in my life, making me intolerant of institutions—especially religious ones—that failed, in my eyes, to be all that they should be. That trait has only intensified with the passing years. I am still painfully idealistic.

Internal struggles and work demands consumed me during what I hoped was my last year at our motherhouse. Some sisters were assigned to manage the various functions there, but it was 1964 and I had been at the Philadelphia motherhouse for four years. I was ready to move on.

A drum-roll of anticipation beat in the background of my days. My study assignment and future professional career would be announced soon. I had no idea what was ahead.

I waited like a child anticipating Christmas morning.

CHAPTER THIRTEEN

NEW KID ON THE BLOCK

In April 1964 I learned that I would attend Catholic University in Washington, DC, to earn a bachelor's degree in nursing. My ego was bruised when three of my peers were selected to study pre-med. Since I perceived nursing to be less intellectually demanding, I assumed my superiors thought I wasn't smart enough to become a doctor. After that prick to my pride, I had to admit that it was probably true—and I wouldn't welcome the long and arduous years of stateside medical studies before going to the missions. Reconciled to my assignment, I paced through the following months like a horse at the starting gate. University studies had fallen outside my reach before joining MMS. I was the first in my family to attend college.

*

Our sister-driver honked the horn as the five of us rode down the winding road of the motherhouse in late August 1964, headed for DC. It had been a good four years in Philly and I felt teary at leaving, but several hours away the small House of Studies awaited me.

We arrived at Sixth and Buchanan Streets NE as the sun slipped below the trees. The hilltop property, with four scattered, nondescript houses, ran down to meet two intersecting roads. A train track and construction yard bordered one street, a wooded area and some rundown houses on the other. My first impression was that my new home was old, isolated, and needed lots of attention. The yard was overgrown and the main house, perched on the top of the rise, resembled a yellowed old woman weathered by life. Inside, mismatched thrift-shop furniture filled the small rooms.

Mother Dengel had bought the property in 1929 for her fledgling group. Its meaningful MMS history and modest appearance warmed my heart toward what would be my home for the next four years. How different it was from the institutional buildings I had left in Philadelphia.

Thirteen sisters would live together in the House of Studies for the

coming school year: three just returned from the missions; two older, home-front sisters; and the rest of us students from several different countries.

I shared a little bungalow at the foot of the hill with two others. We walked back and forth, up and down, in sun, rain, and snow for meals, chapel, recreation, and sleeping. I liked the tiny pinches of inconvenience as practices of my vow of poverty.

I'm the one with the flying veil.

For freshman orientation at Catholic University, I walked the mile to campus along the train track. My long gray habit and blue veil stood out in the indistinguishable mass of young guys and gals wearing their requisite beanies and twirling yo-yos, a freshman ritual I was spared. Though I was four years older than most of the incoming students, I still shared their "new kid on the block" nervousness. They were uncomfortable with me in my nun's habit until I initiated conversations, and then they opened up and were warm and friendly.

I missed not having a sister companion from my community to share this experience, but it gave me more independence, and being alone made me more approachable to other students.

The electric atmosphere on the campus enchanted me: clusters of students chatting on the paths, sitting on the grass, clutching campus maps as they scanned the daunting stone buildings to find their classes. Men and women of all ages swirled around me as I stood in the midst of it all, trying to absorb that new environment. The palpable energy and sense of a new freedom pulsed through me, beating a rhythm in my body.

Because many religious orders had houses of study in the area, the campus swarmed with pairs of nuns who seemed stuck to each other in a medley of black-and-white habits. Seminarians strode along in their traditional black, ankle-length cassocks. Priests and nuns, lay students, and faculty intermingled, like a modern dance flowing across campus.

After years of all-female living, interacting with so many men threw me off center. As I got to know more fellows, especially the seminarians, I sensed that beneath the facade of asking about homework assignments or the next hootenanny, they sought my company. I worried that I felt pleasure from their attention.

My freshman year covered general requirements as a prelude to my nursing courses: philosophy, psychology, sociology, and history, among others, and I savored the potpourri of disciplines.

In sociology we studied drug addiction. For one of my projects, an MMS supporter and a conflicted man with ties to organized crime was a frequent visitor to our house. He arranged for me to interview Don, an ex-con drug addict whom he knew from being in prison together.

Don and I met on campus one spring afternoon and sat on a tree-shaded bench for two hours while I interviewed him. He was a gentle hulk of a man struggling to find solid ground after his many falls. Just to hear of the deprivations and brutality of his childhood made me understand why a person would attempt to escape from such damaging memories though drugs. He unhinged my guileless existence with accounts of abuse he endured in prison.

After two hours of immersion in his life story I could offer no more than a hug when we stood to go our separate ways. He, however, had gifted me with an understanding that would serve as an always needed reminder— never presume to judge another human being.

CHAPTER FOURTEEN

EMPATHY

My nursing theory and clinical practice rotated though the specialties of medicine and surgery, pediatrics, obstetrics, psychiatry, and public health at numerous medical facilities in the city. Those first two years I wore a white habit, the same style as worn in the missions. It made me feel like an angelic Clara Barton, and I fantasized wearing it in a mission hospital soon.

During my last two years at the university, the MMS had changed into regular women's clothing, so I wore an ordinary white uniform and an impractical nurse's cap precariously balanced on my head, which was always sliding off when I bent over.

But more than trying to balance a slipping cap, nursing stretched my boundaries of caring and competence in ways I could not have foreseen.

I had been caring for a young mother of two with terminal cancer. She was dying in pain while I sat with her frail hand in mine, only able to offer my silent presence. I spoke of her in a letter to my parents: "I can hardly bear her suffering, so how can she?"

My early days at the hospital were both difficult and deeply satisfying when I could make a difference for patients and their families. I still hadn't learned many nursing procedures, but my contact with patients was what I looked forward to each day: comforting a disoriented elderly woman, using jokes to ease the embarrassment of a man being bathed by a young nun, assuring a boy how brave he was as I gently cleaned his incision.

For one week after my day shift ended, I sat with a four-year-old Shirley Temple look-alike with an advanced Wilm's tumor, a rare childhood cancer. Treatments had stopped, hope for a cure abandoned. Hovering over her bed I hummed songs and stroked her arm, as I had done with my younger siblings, until her parents came from work. When they arrived, I watched them paste smiles on their faces for her, hiding their grief.

I waited until I left the room to cry.

During my psychiatry affiliation, I found the anxiety of a new patient could be calmed if I spent extra time helping him or her get oriented and meet other patients in the daunting dayroom. My outgoing personality could be put to use in easing transitions for those who felt so alone and alienated.

Empathy is a potent antidote to the fear and vulnerability typical of many medical institutions where patients' emotional needs go uncared for. The power and poignancy of ordinary people with all their many faces, all their histories, were present with them in their hospital beds. As a young nurse, I wanted to bring all of myself to aid in their recovery from whatever illness or disability limited their lives.

I was beginning to understand that my heart would be wounded time and again when my loving care was not enough to alleviate my patients' suffering. I was yet to learn that my own limited abilities and the nursing profession itself did not have the influence and sway over the body and spirit that I naively thought they would.

And I grew to hate hospital nursing.

I was caring for a scruffy alcoholic with a scraggly beard and advanced cirrhosis of the liver. A young intern came in and told me to hold the man's legs down while he inserted a tube down the man's nose and into his stomach. I had never witnessed this procedure before. He did it without any anesthesia. The patient writhed in pain and thrashed about as the doctor tried to push the tube into his throat. While the intern was obviously nervous, he was shockingly rough with the patient. I stifled my impulse to scream at him to stop—but I couldn't, for I was at the bottom of the hospital pecking order.

Blood began spurting from the engorged vessels in the patient's esophagus, and he was gagging on it. Frustrated and shaken, the doctor pulled out the tube, threw it on the bed, and stomped out, telling me to clean up the bloodied patient. I shook with pent-up rage: for the heartless treatment of that patient, for the overworked and stressed intern, and for myself who stood by, unable to help either of them.

I managed to do the required hospital tasks because I had to, but I was so sensitive to the pain of others, it became my own. I hated doing any procedures that hurt people.

Further, I resented reprimands by the head nurse for spending too much time talking to patients and their families, especially since I intentionally did so. Many of them needed attention, someone to listen to their fears, to their unmet needs. I disliked being constrained in how I practiced nursing and wanted to be able to set my own priorities.

Lack of sufficient practice with technical skills such as drawing blood or inserting a catheter added to my discomfort. The university nursing programs offered less hands-on experience than the three-year hospital programs of that time. That interfered with my sense of competence, a core psychic need of mine, and caused me a diminished enjoyment of nursing.

My later nursing career veered away from the institutional setting to the
independence of public health nursing, a better match for my personality and my professional understanding that prevention is generally
preferable to treatment.

My empathetic nature also placed me in a situation that slipped
into ambiguity.

I'd been assigned to the hospital's medical wing, where one of my
patients was a quiet man in his forties who spoke with a strong Eastern
European accent. As I was finishing a routine check of his vital signs,
the doctor came in and told Mr. M. that his condition was terminal.
There was nothing more they could do. I had backed up against the
wall, fearing that my presence was an intrusion on an intensely personal
moment. After the doctor left Mr. M. broke down, his shoulders shaking
with sobs. I rushed to his bedside and held him in my arms, stroking
his head as he cried on my shoulder—a devastated man-child. After his
tears were spent, he spoke in a whisper, *"What will I do now?"* I listened
to his anguish for several minutes. Then he wanted to rest, so I left to
attend to my other patients but my body was trembling. I ducked into
the restroom to pull myself together, worried that I had been unprofes-
sional, had crossed some nurse-patient, male-nun line. *Had I been too
tender, too intimate . . . too . . . what?* I didn't know.

The day after that incident I was assigned to the other end of the unit,
but I sought out Mr. M. on my lunch break. A smile spread on his
otherwise sad face when I entered his room. We both felt the palpable
connection between us after such a profound moment the day before.

Before I went off my shift I stopped by to see him again. He was like a
young boy when I entered. His eyes dropped, but he kept smiling and
said he was glad I came by.

The sweetness between us was new for me.

The next day, Mr. M. was leaving the hospital to die. I avoided him all
day until we met in the hallway as he was leaving. There was a wistful
look in his eyes when he said, "I will think of you often." I wanted to say

the same to him but couldn't—I was a nun. I struggled for appropriate words, feared I might slip over some inchoate line defined by my vow of celibacy. Though wanting to hug him good-bye, I shook his hand.

Later that night, in tears, I confessed in my journal my sense of loss and separation:

> Preparing for sleep tonight my heart is breaking as I think about Mr. M. I see how limited and constrained my life is. I offer the pain in my heart to God. I realized today how separate we all are—how I can't be all things to all people, can't reach the depths I desire in my relationships. As close as people may be to me, there are still borders I can't breach. I wonder if even the Bible's definition of marriage, "They shall become one flesh," can bridge the boundary of self?

As I moved through my early twenties at Catholic University and the various medical settings of my nursing practice, I was increasingly aware of men's attraction to me. I wondered how those moments would be different, go in another direction, if I weren't a nun. I knew I would feel freer in my interactions with men, I was certain of that . . . but I *was* a nun, so those questions were always pressed away, like flowers tucked between the pages of a book to be dried out—and forgotten.

CHAPTER FIFTEEN

LOSS AND GAIN

The entire community of Medical Mission Sisters was to hold a Chapter soon, a momentous gathering of representatives from around the world to plan our future and institute needed changes. Every sister was invited to send in her suggestions, and I had so many it was taking me hours to record all my thoughts on paper. I was thoroughly convinced that we were in a period of significant historical change. I believed that many of the Church's practices were untenable for modern times, the wealth and formality of Rome foreign to Jesus' vision. The Church had to adapt itself, or whole sectors of humankind would lose faith in the institution. We also needed to change as individuals. In my view, much in American society and religious life lacked a soul.

During those years when my intellectual and personal boundaries were stretched by my academic studies and nursing practice, Pope John XXIII's Vatican Council sent gusts through the entire Catholic world. He initiated a new vision for the Church that opened medieval doors and windows, letting in the fresh air of modernization, but also creating huge upheavals in the lives of religious women—and in mine. The new directive from Rome to women's communities focused on the formation of young women for an "incarnational" religious life—finding God in the world and being a part of that world, not separate, as in the monastic tradition we inherited. The document addressed the importance of a mature decision to enter religious life, not the flock of eighteen-year-olds, like me, who had been entering around that time.

Some women's religious communities were resistant to those fresh perspectives while others, like Medical Mission Sisters, wanted to be freed from irrelevant practices to focus on the essential Christian message, buried under centuries of institutional accretions.

The many expectations and behaviors pressed upon Catholic nuns up to that time had often burdened our sisters who struggled with culturally challenging medical work in countries that were predominately Hindu, Muslim, or Buddhist.

In response to the voluminous documents flowing from the Vatican Council, Medical Mission Sisters began preparation for our International Chapter of reassessment in 1967. It was an exhilarating and disturbing upheaval for individual sisters, as well as for the leadership of the entire community.

In February 1966 my Washington community of twelve traveled back to Philadelphia to our motherhouse for a "State of the Union" address by the superior of the American province, just back from preparatory Chapter sessions. So many exciting ideas were coming out of their meetings—ideas many of us had discussed and promoted.

One of the fun events that weekend was a fashion show to explore what we might wear if we no longer used the traditional, body-covering habits. They were such a challenge in the tropics and strange to peoples of other cultures, let alone to our own. I had always thought our unusual outfits were a sign to others of our commitment to God, but now I felt they just made nuns look odd and unapproachable. How many penguin jokes did I have to hear?

After an introduction to the show, one sister after another came into the room modeling proposed outfits. How strange to see their legs for the first time. Milling around later, it began to feel natural to see them in contemporary clothes and feminine hairdos. Some members favored modified habits or dark-colored suits, but I and many others wanted to wear modest women's clothes. It would be so much simpler; our dress could be adapted to the cultures in which we worked.

Though it seemed an external change, what we wore unleashed unexpected reactions.

One week before our official launch into regular women's wear in the spring of 1966, my mother arrived at our DC house with a carload of donated dresses. Her hairdresser friend, Betty, came to remediate our then hidden and neglected hair.

After they left we roamed stores for slips, shoes and stockings, and hair products. The next Monday we all made our grand entrance into chapel with curls bobbing and heels clicking.

Most of my friends on campus didn't recognize me in street clothes, so I felt invisible. They looked right at me and walked on. From others I got the shocked, "Oh, my God!" Others sidled up and whispered, "Did you leave the convent?" I also had naughty comments from some of the males I knew, suggesting they enjoyed seeing more of me.

I felt comfortable . . . felt like myself. I hated to think about going back into the habit if our wardrobe experimentation wasn't approved after that trial period. But once let loose in cool and comfortable clothing, there was no turning back.

I am second on the right in our new look.

When I had the opportunity to wear regular clothes, I was confronted by the fact that hidden beneath the layers of fabric was a woman's body. It changed my sense of myself and liberated me, but it also opened a world of interactions for which I wasn't prepared. Losing the habit and being exposed as a twenty-three-year-old female was complicated by the widespread stirrings of sexual liberation in American society. Both religious and secular books and lectures promoted the popular psychology of healthy egos and whole personality development. They all contributed to a heightened self-awareness and pinched, like tight shoes, my earlier easy embrace of celibacy.

Various entries in my journal from 1966 to 1968 attest to the tension between my vows and a broadening understanding of the human condition. A great challenge lay in integrating my new awareness that holiness and human wholeness were not only compatible, but the same.

I had watched the play *Little Moon of Alban* on TV—about a young Irish nun told to care for a British soldier. He fell in love with her, begged her to leave the convent and marry him. She loved him too, but remained a nun. I thought it plausible that he would fall in love with a woman who nursed him back to health, but felt strongly that the sister should have seen what was happening and removed herself from the situation before it had progressed so far.

How naive I was about the powerful pull of romantic love and pheromones. In my opinion, the young nun was wrong for not protecting herself from the temptation of an attractive man. The future would take me to task for my quick judgment.

During the late sixties I heard many stories of sisters leaving religious life, even some of my MMS friends. An entire community of sisters in Los Angeles, California, left the Church over its patriarchal stance. More often individuals left because they experienced a personal love for a man—often a priest—or wanted the option of marriage for themselves. It saddened me that they chose to abandon our compelling vision.

We were all realizing that the nature of change brings both gain and loss.

Out of the protective habit, I did not know how to react to men's attraction to me—at times flattering, but most often uncomfortable. Each time a man related to me as a woman, not a nun, something rock-solid in me was slowly worn down, like water drops on stone.

By now I was also admitting in the privacy of my journals that attractions didn't flow just one way. My instinctively affectionate nature needed to learn how to act where men were involved. I wrote one night after an evening with a group of my sisters:

One of the sisters was talking about another one whom she felt behaved differently when she was around men. I have to evaluate myself in this regard. I do enjoy men's company and occasionally even feel an attraction, but I have to control those feelings. Do I ever invite something more in my heterosexual contacts? Lord, help me to see clearly.

During those years of radical transformations, three years had rushed by. It was time to renew my vows for two more years. The community was willing to keep me, and I didn't want to leave, despite my niggling questions about celibacy.

On the evening of the renewal of my vows toward the close of summer 1966 I rested in a place of peace and ease, a bird in its nest. In the previous few months I had not strayed from my desire to remain a Medical Mission Sister. I renewed my vows full of all the love I'd stored up over the years. I was full of hope that the Chapter would approve the changes necessary to allow our religious life to become a full, uncluttered means to living the true Christian message of love and compassion for all. During the ceremony I spoke my heartfelt words: "I renew my vows in gratitude for the joys of six years in the Society, and in faith in the unknown."

CHAPTER SIXTEEN

FALLING WALLS

The energy and enthusiasm generated by life at Catholic University and the structure-shaking 1960s percolated around and in me. New ventures brought more dimensions to my skills and personality, expanding my sense of what it meant to be a religious woman. Everything seemed possible if I focused on my authentic impulses to do good.

Leadership came naturally to me, perhaps because of the "oldest daughter" syndrome, and it combined with my persistent tendency to want to make things better than they were.

I initiated a student-faculty dialogue in the nursing department to address some of our complaints. The idea was initially met with resistance and anger, but after I sold the idea to the dean, we had a successful series of exchanges over several months.

I also felt strongly that our student MMS needed a voice in our community's governing body, since our particular set of concerns were not represented. I advocated for that via letters sent to sister students around the US and the American District Assembly. The position was approved and I was elected to be the first student representative at subsequent districtwide meetings.

Sister Clare and I broke into the clerical conference, an organization of all the seminaries in the DC area—and another patriarchal wall came crashing down. Women have always been treated as second-class citizens in the Church, as they are in the larger world. Powerful enough to be blamed for man's fall, yet called the weaker sex, women's true strength and profound gifts have been suppressed for most of human history by the patriarchal system of dominance, which functions like the immune system, denying or destroying anything that doesn't look like itself. This ruthless mindset is rampant everywhere in the world, but as I grew into my own sense of competence, I sought equality for myself and other women.

Sister Clare and I wanted the seminaries to open their doors to nuns so we could benefit from their excellent series of lectures and discussions. Perhaps they wanted to protect themselves from the incursion of tempting females, but we thought it unfair for them to keep such good programs to themselves.

Uninvited, we showed up at one of their steering committee meetings. After they recovered from the shock of seeing our unfamiliar female faces enter the room, the chairman rose to the occasion and said they were grateful for our interest.

On the way home afterwards we both laughed; each time either of us raised our hand to suggest something, we were immediately recognized with a "Yes, Sister? What do *you* think?" and they agreed with our request to open their educational programs to women religious. We had won them over to our logic.

Another sister and I started a summer project in inner-city Washington that kept expanding. We worked with ten neglected tykes in the morning. I saw so much in those kids that I'd never noticed before: scared facial expressions and unvoiced needs. Then the gradual relaxing of their tight little bodies when I'd hug or pat them with affection.

We started making door-to-door home visits and health surveys in their neighborhood. The people were surprisingly responsive to us. It helped me overcome my fear of being a white woman walking those predominantly black inner-city streets. The degree of poverty was foreign to me. My own wall had to come down—the one that made me think we were separate. Working that summer in the city gave me a new comfort with myself and people I met, whatever our differences.

Of course, my days and emotions were not all satisfying and enjoyable. A 1967 entry reflected the tidal shifts of time in my moods:

> Here it is again, another year used up. I'm in my bedroom watching heavy sheets of snow fall outside. This stilling weather is appropriate for my retreat day. The snow reminds me that I need to be uncovering, not covering over, truth. I've felt the need to confront things building up inside me. My days go along smoothly, and then—wham!—something confronts me head-on. My understanding of what life is about keeps changing with each new experience, and then all the disparate pieces need to be rearranged to fit together. It's such a laborious process, this living and growing.

> I just turned twenty-five last month. Who am I and where am I going with all the activities I've gotten involved with? Am I losing my center with all these external involvements? What I most want is to love everyone who touches my lifelines. That is the heart of it all, isn't it?

My relationships with campus friends continued to deepen, and I continued to wrestle with my male relationships. I didn't want to misinterpret their friendliness, and I didn't know how to be an open, caring person without it being wrongly interpreted.

But with all the activities and intensive soul-searching, my four years at the university slipped into the past while I wasn't watching.

I had a stimulating and supportive community at our bustling House of Studies and a wide circle of friends on campus and in the city. Intertwined with my earnest nursing practice and deepening spiritual growth were breakthrough moments of humor and its offspring, laughter.

One Holy Thursday we celebrated the Eucharist upstairs in the chapel and then proceeded downstairs to our dining room, singing *Shalom*. I had planned a festive Easter meal in the style of the Jewish Passover and had baked unleavened bread. As we sat around our dining table, the priest celebrant began a solemn prayer while he prepared to break and pass the bread—but it was like a rock. After several efforts to break off small pieces with his strong hands, he resorted to tapping, then pounding the hardened loaf on the edge of the dining table. When it finally cracked, we feared it was the table, not the bread, that broke. Father's face crumpled. I wanted to hide. Everyone took in a breath—and then we all burst into laughter. We skipped the rest of the ritual and enjoyed the dinner. Father took a piece of the rock back to his community so they would believe him when he tried to describe the failed sharing of Passover bread at the sisters' house.

Those four years in Washington, DC were among the happiest times in my life. Even without the habit, my accidental reflection in a mirror—like the silver vase of years before—assured me I was a Medical Mission Sister.

CHAPTER SEVENTEEN

THE BIG YES

After graduating from Catholic University in May 1968, I spent a July week in silence and prayer at the Philadelphia motherhouse in preparation for my final vows in August. It was a time of probing the decision before me—at twenty-five, I was about to promise the rest of my life to a path that would often ask more than I felt I could do.

Of the three vows, celibacy had the greatest focus for a young woman my age. In my journals, I was digging deep into the what-if's and why's.

I know sexuality is an integral part of every person. So what does remaining a virgin for God mean, if sex is such an inherent and profound dimension of being human? To choose to pass up that intimacy is to say that there is something more to our humanity. It's like leaving a life jacket on the beach to tell the boatsman you trust his skill. The life jacket—or celibacy—is not what's necessary, but what it says of your trust. God doesn't want my virginity, he wants my faith. But what happens to the personal development of a celibate? How do I honor my God-given body, my female sexuality?

My early formative years as a nun had taught me to hide my body, not only from the eyes of others but even from myself. There were few mirrors in our houses, and I had to sew down all my bra cups to flatten my breasts. In my two years in the novitiate, underwear was a loose-fitting one-piece garment made from coarse flour sacks, some still bearing a company stamp. The unspoken yet clear message was that our bodies were not for ourselves but were to be used in service of others.

Fortunately, by the late sixties those petty practices of modesty and self-denial disappeared. Those of us trained in that earlier mentality gradually had to evolve into a new sense of ourselves, our bodies, our womanhood. For many sisters, it was a divide that they were not able or chose not to jump across.

Working out the fine balance between being a sexual person and a celibate was more a theoretical dilemma than a practical one for me . . . then. I was clear that the desire to serve was far more powerful a drive than hormones. I was a committed Medical Mission Sister.

But I did shine a light on my motives during mental interrogations of myself throughout those retreat days.

> How can I be loved as a person, a woman? How can I express my love for people, even men, without trespassing on my celibate commitment?
>
> What would it be like to find a like-minded man who would love me and share a desire to work overseas? But why am I asking that? Am I being drawn to something outside Medical Mission Sisters?—or just taking a last look at what I am leaving behind?
>
> Why should I make my final vows in August? Because I'm so connected to this community of gifted sisters and our shared faith in the Christian message, because many people look up to me, and because our medical mission work is so needed . . . And finally, because this present life is temporary.
>
> Why should I leave? Sometimes, I don't feel strong enough to thrive in this demanding environment. I need so much emotional support. I get too

*introspective ... and so much time and effort is
consumed by the endless organizational aspects of
living together in a large group.*

My ongoing ruminations led me to intuit a central truth. I couldn't let
any man, or work, or my community of sisters—any *one* thing—become
my all. Deep within, driving me forward, was a yearning for intimacy
with an ineffable God.

I hungered for an undivided heart.

On the eve of my final commitment in August 1968, I wrote:

*Tomorrow is as serious as a wedding day, but I'll never
have one. What a strange woman I am not to sorrow
over the fact but only feel a twinge of regret that my
parents won't get to celebrate my wedding ... Well,
perhaps a bit for myself, too. Yet tomorrow means for
always; always the effort required to live with other
women in community, always the unending medical
work, always prayer. Though I don't know what's
ahead, I have to choose it. I can't go back now, for the
pattern has been set. My eight years of preparation
point toward a future as a Medical Mission Sister. So
here I am—and here I go into tomorrow!*

Kneeling at the altar rail before the bishop on August fifteenth in a ritual
that mirrored all the past ceremonies that had brought me to that point,
the words I composed and then spoke came from the deepest place I
could plumb within myself:

*I, Sister Aimee, come to this day of decision supported
by my family, friends, and sisters. With joy and hope, I
give my entire life to working out the Kingdom of God.
I entrust myself—all that I am and shall be—to this
community of sisters and those they serve throughout*

the world. I choose to share in our Medical Mission, to live motivated by the Gospel spirit, and according to our constitution. Amen!

I said my big YES that day, walked across the threshold, and moved all the luggage that was me into the house called religious life.

CHAPTER EIGHTEEN

AT LAST

In the months after graduation I worked the evening shift on a medical-surgical unit at a Philadelphia hospital while living again at the motherhouse. I needed many hours of practice for my poorly honed nursing skills before I went overseas.

But after working just a brief time at the hospital, I was asked to join a formation team for incoming postulants, as well as the vocation team. Those teams replaced the past role of a superior. I was also asked to create a month-long trip around the Western US—in the middle of winter—to meet with potential applicants and to promote our work in each city or town I visited. Entrusted with such weighty responsibilities at the motherhouse, I feared they might keep me there rather than give me an overseas mission assignment.

I had expressed a desire to go to Africa and lived in a state of suspension until I learned my fate. The community's mantra was: "A Medical Missionary goes wherever she is sent, to do the work assigned, not counting the cost to self." But the changes introduced by our recent 1967 Chapter encouraged sisters to be attentive to their talents and interests—and mine was Africa. I can't explain why—it's like love—it has no reason.

I made a solitary, week-long retreat on the Chesapeake Bay in May 1969. It was a significant time of reflection and revealed how my thoughts continued to evolve.

> I am drawn to understand the meaning of this vow of poverty—to find how to live simply, to keep my needs down and my possessions few, so that I can bite into the truest things of life.

Lying here on the pier, I began thinking about the Kingdom of God and it struck me that maybe the "Kingdom" is reality, and each person only has a small inscape into it, but the closer we come to knowing reality, the closer we are to the Kingdom.

As a young nun preparing to leave the nest of the familiar, I longed to ground myself in what I called "reality"—out of recognition, perhaps, that I was too idealistic and had been protected by my family and religious community from the hard-boned lives of so many other people I'd met in the past years. I wanted to be an authentic Medical Mission Sister. Fully human. Fully Christian. Fully committed to loving, generous service. I wanted to be ready to face the daunting realities at the other end of a mission assignment.

In September, during my ninth year in the community and after one year of final vows, my overseas mission was announced. Not only was I going to Africa, but I had been assigned to a new MMS venture called the Cultural Orientation Program Experiment (COPE), but generally referred to as the Pilot Project. Two countries where we had missions were designated to host the program: Dacca, East Pakistan, and Malawi, East-Central Africa.

What glorious news for me. Without really knowing much of what the project would involve, I knew I was going to the missions. At last!

So much preparation had to be undertaken to get ready, but a priority was to send the following letter to all my family and friends, after I had called my parents to share my happiness with them.

MEDICAL MISSION SISTERS
Philadelphia 11, Pa.
October 8, 1969

Please excuse this form letter, but it is the quickest way to share my good news with everyone who matters to me. At last I am going to Malawi, East-Central Africa. I'm extremely happy!

Since graduating with a BSN degree, I've been doing nursing and personnel work for my religious community in Philadelphia. During this time, a Pilot Project was being planned to study how to provide language and cultural orientation for sisters going to our missions. Up to now, sufficient time to learn the language and the culture of a country wasn't available to newly arrived members; they started working in the hospital or clinic shortly after they reached their destination. This Pilot Project is going to test a theory of enculturation for the future.

Malawi, ranked as the second poorest country in the world, will be my home in the coming years. It is a small country, the shape of an appendix, wedged between Zambia and Portuguese East Africa.

Currently there are twenty-three Dutch MMS in Phalombe, Malawi. I am the only American going there along with three young Filipina sisters. The sisters staff a 100-bed bush hospital, with a nursing and midwifery school, and several outlying clinics.

My plans are slowly taking shape. I will leave for England in early December where I hope to spend some time with Sister Clare, a MMS friend from my Catholic University days. I must be in the Netherlands by December 5 to begin a six week orientation to the Dutch way of life, since I will have not one but two cultures to assimilate in Malawi!

I also hope to visit some American friends living in Germany while in Europe. In January I will fly to Africa. Anyone have an old pith helmet around?

Finally, after nine years of preparation, I shall find out what it is that's been calling me since I was eight years old.

Please be close to me in these last two months—I suspect I shall need to believe in that.

Stowaways will be welcomed,

Sister Aimee

I was allowed to visit my family and relatives for Thanksgiving dinner in 1969, our last time all together until only God knew, for I was to leave soon for Europe on my way to Africa.

Back l-r: Gina, Johnny, Mike, Dot, Ronnie
Front: Dan, Dad, Sam, Me, Mom, Tom.

We had a family picture taken; my parents and all my siblings. We did not know that it would be the last photo of our entire family together. Even Sam, the dog, was in the picture, hogging the camera. My family's sweet good-night kisses were mixed with briny tears.

Once back at the motherhouse, I turned to my journal, as I always did, to sort through my emotions from the evening.

> Strange how I react to the encroaching separation;
> I need to be alone here in my room. It's the same
> withdrawal from the pain of separation I felt before
> leaving home for Medical Mission Sisters at age
> seventeen. Am I a loner at heart, drawn to a solitary
> room when my emotions pull me me into their depth?
>
> Strange too, that so many people mean so much to me,
> yet not enough to keep me here. There is no person, no
> thing, no love greater than the unknown that calls me
> on in search of itself.
>
> My hope for this life ahead is to rub noses with
> the truest elements of reality—but I fear that my
> expectations are too big to squeeze into my own five-
> and ten-cent self. Perhaps I'm a small person who needs
> the grand stage of international work to feel there's

something significant about me, a working-class girl from Philadelphia. I'm afraid of doing the common thing, in the usual fashion, for fear I'll be lost in the crowd before I'm even found.

To be all that I want to be, is one thing; to be all that I am able to be, quite another. Maybe my time in Africa will be the chance to forge the difference, discern that elusive reality I search for, when my tiny world meets the larger one.

Will I be still standing at the end?

CHAPTER NINETEEN

LEAVING HOME

It was a biting cold night outside the Philadelphia airport on December 2, 1969. Inside the concourse, my family surrounded me like a bulwark, as though to fend off my approaching departure.

Earlier that day I had said good-bye to the sisters at our Philadelphia motherhouse. The members of my community understood the joy of my leaving for a mission assignment, but for my family, especially my parents, it felt like a chasm thrown between us. Africa was terribly far away . . . and I had a one-way ticket.

We ate our last supper in an airport eatery where I ordered a hamburger and milk shake, my final taste of an American favorite, but anxiety made it hard to swallow. My food choked down, we migrated to the departure gate where we milled around, straining for jokes to lighten the heavy mood. It was hard to look into anyone's eyes for long, especially Mom's and Dad's.

Finally an overhead voice shattered the tension: "Pan Am Flight #789 now boarding." A flurry of arms grabbed me, and kisses peppered my face as I pulled away.

Leaving my family and country released a hailstorm of feelings, but after almost a decade of preparation for this, the fear cramping my belly was tempered by excitement. I was on my way to realize my long-desired chance to serve in another country.

Following the jagged line of passengers over the tarmac to the plane, I felt so alone. I buoyed my slipping spirit by humming "The Impossible Dream" from *Man of La Mancha*.

After wrestling my rock-heavy bags up the plane's steps, I bumped down the aisle to my seat. *My* seat—how comforting to have something that was mine when letting go of so much. Once buckled up, I peered out and caught the silhouette of my family clinging to each other, a human skyline framed by the terminal's window. They couldn't see me, yet I waved frantically, longing for one last good-bye.

The plane groaned in retreat, lurched down the runway, made a U-turn, and picked up speed as it rushed past the terminal. The ties to my familiar world snapped. Emotions held back earlier escaped in sobs that I tried to stifle in my coat collar. The man next to me in the middle seat stiffened, pulled his arm away from our common armrest and burrowed into a magazine. The woman in the aisle seat furtively stared at me. I wanted to tell her that no, in spite of my erupting grief, I had not lost my entire family in a fire or endured some other tragedy—I was just leaving home.

After five minutes of unrelenting choking, coughing, and nose-blowing, I reclaimed my composure and focused on the seven-hour flight to London, the first of several long layovers—England, the Netherlands, and Germany—on my passage to Malawi.

Having read the emergency card from the seat pocket for fifteen minutes, I still had no idea what it said. Nothing seemed to penetrate my numbed mind until the pilot's voice captured my attention with his description of the locations we were flying over: Long Island, Boston, Cape Cod. Nostalgia tapped me on the shoulder; I had camped on the Cape just that past summer with two other sisters.

Turbulence over Newfoundland rattled the plane—and me—but not long after, we slipped off the edge of the North American continent, and I was floating through night's black sea. A British flight attendant offered me a tantalizing menu, but my emotional belly was too full. The newness of my first transcontinental flight and thoughts of my final destination were enough to chew on.

Unsettled sleep finally came. Hours into the flight, a chipper male voice interrupted my drugged-like dozing. "We're passing over Belfast,

Ireland, and will land at Heathrow within the hour." My mind rattled awake—where am I? My window reflected a fuzzy face against the wall of darkness outside—and who am I?

I went to the rear bathroom to freshen up: combed out the quirks in my hair, tried to pull my wrinkled self together. Filling out the entry permit back in my seat confirmed that there was no turning back.

The herd of weary travelers disembarked into a dismal English morning and a waiting bus. A heavily made-up woman reeking of liquor wedged beside me and asked, "Where's thish bus takin' ush?" Guessing, I suggested to my bleary companion that it would take us to the terminal, an opinion that prompted her to proclaim, "You're vury, vury smart, Missy." I thought it funny that I, a "wet behind the ears" traveler, was asked for advice.

Once inside the building, not knowing where to go in Heathrow's beehive, I followed the swarm through the halls. My first taste of relief came when I passed through the last queue, collected my luggage, and arrived in the outer terminal with my belongings piled on a cart.

My virginal passport bore its first stamp.

Clare, a Medical Mission Sister and friend from our student days in Washington, DC was to meet me, but she was nowhere in the crowd of foreign faces. I was a lost waif in that great hall of people, who all seemed to know where they were going. A multitude of nationalities were evident in the faces and dress swirling around me. Loud British voices assaulted my ears with announcements of train departure platforms and arriving flights. Countless advertisements and airport signs bewildered me; arrows pointed me in a hundred different directions.

My throat tightened as I searched the faces in the unfriendly brush of bodies for just one that I knew. Desperate to calm myself, I stopped and stood in the midst of it all and spent several minutes digging through my purse as though searching for something. The crowd ebbed and flowed around me as though I wasn't there.

Minutes felt like hours. I had to do something to control the anxiety overtaking me, so I entered a phone booth to call my missing friend. *Oh no, I need English coins to use the phone!*

At the exchange desk, wanting to show the confidence of a native, I contrived a British accent during the transaction that changed five dollars into two pounds, two shillings. I suspect the clerk knew I was a fake.

My next challenge was the phone itself. How did it work? While I fumbled inside the booth like an inept Superman, a knock on the glass alerted me to the apologetic face of my friend. Our excited words bumped into each other as we whooped and danced in each other's arms.

Clare, blessed with an infectious laugh and effusive personality, escorted me into London's pale morning. As I waited with my luggage for her to bring the car, I chatted with another bystander, still using the infectious British accent. My role-playing reminded me of high school and how I would pretend to have a limp or struggle to speak in limited English to a bus driver or ticket seller—or anyone who didn't know me—to see if they would believe my ruse. It was the actress in me.

My first sights of life outside the airport exploded with British icons: bobbies fortressed in their long black coats, too-tall hats, and billy clubs motioned walkers along; red double-decker buses swished past, bodies clinging to both ends; taxis that reminded me of hearses honked their way through the traffic lanes. I was in London!

A car slid to the curb with Clare behind a misplaced steering wheel. Driving down the wrong side of streets headed for the village of Osterley, I clung to my seat, dizzy and disoriented.

After a forty-five minute ride, a right turn onto Thornbury Road and a twist into the circular gravel driveway landed us in front of the Medical Mission Sisters' house, an ordinary, cement box of a building devoid of the quaint charm of cottages we had passed.

Several British sisters welcomed me with outstretched arms and pecks on my cheek as I entered the foyer. After the greetings, Clare proposed a cup of hot coffee and escorted me downstairs to the dark, chilly kitchen where the cook, Annie, was hopping around and chirping little songs. When she noticed me, she said, "Ow ish yah, luvvy?" I was deeply embarrassed that I couldn't understand one word of her cockney English. It was to be my first of many linguistic challenges.

That evening I joined everyone in the chapel and prayed in gratitude for the comfort of being surrounded by women of my religious community. Afterwards the noisy chatter of all fourteen sisters accompanied a simple supper of soup, coarse bread, and hot tea.

Clare invited me upstairs once I visited with the other sisters. Brightly colored sixties-era posters proclaiming liberation as the new spiritual quest plastered her bedroom walls. We talked until 2:00 a.m., going deeper into our soul spaces with each passing hour.

At one point Clare's face tightened. "I'm thinking about leaving Medical Mission Sisters," she said. "Since I've been in England after my studies in the States, I realize this aging community is stuck in the past. I feel like I'll die if I stay here."

My insides crumbled. I was about to beg her to return to our more progressive American community when she added, "I've met a man, a college professor, and he loves me ... and I think I love him. The contrast between my times with Stephen and when I'm here with the sisters has become unbearable."

What could I say? This was beyond my own personal experience, though I knew several sisters who had left in recent years ... but, no, not my dear friend whom I had always admired. I was disheartened by her news, and after the initial shock, I felt a strange disconnection. The choice before her formed a fissure between us. Perhaps that feeling of estrangement was my way of protecting myself from the pain of friends leaving a life to which I was still deeply devoted, like mates abandoning a ship we had all been sailing together. The only words that surfaced in that moment were that I would pray she made a wise decision.

Though her revelation the previous night weighed on me, Clare and I

Tower of London.

enjoyed playing tourists for a few hours the next day. Traveling by the Underground, I gawked at the famous station names that flew past: Charing Cross . . . Piccadilly . . . Wimbledon . . . Westminster. We toured the Tower of London and I pranced over London Bridge, thinking of that childhood nursery rhyme.

Returning to Osterley just in time for a quick attack on my suitcase, I said a grateful good-bye to the sisters and jumped in the car for a rushed ride to Heathrow airport and my flight to Amsterdam. I gave Clare a hard, long hug, not knowing if I would ever see her again. She did leave Medical Mission Sisters. I met her again, briefly, in 1971, when she was enjoying her new life as a single woman in fast-paced London.

On the shuttle bus to my plane, a young chap kept staring at me. I was not used to being ogled by strange men. Since I was not wearing a habit, he had no clues I was a nun. Once we boarded, he chose a seat next to me, so I quickly alerted him to my religious status. My discomfort turned to pleasure when he mentioned he was returning from a tour of Africa and had visited Malawi. I explained that I was going there and described the work of the Medical Mission Sisters. It was fortuitous to meet someone who had been there—and returned alive.

Throughout the flight to Amsterdam I deprived my companion of any peace with staccato questions about the country and people of my future home. We talked nonstop until we reached the terminal and had to go our separate ways. His prolonged handshake as we said good-bye told me he felt the same Velcro pull I did.

Walking away, I was on my own again.

CHAPTER TWENTY

GOING DUTCH

The customs process at Schiphol Airport went smoothly and I traded my pounds for guilders with the casual air of an experienced traveler. I didn't need to fake a Dutch accent—nor would I have been able to.

Two robust, English-speaking Dutch sisters greeted me on the other side of the arrival partition. Keeping the conversation going on our night drive to Heerlen, a small town three hours south, they told me the three Filipina Medical Mission Sisters in the Pilot Project had already arrived, described the community members with whom I would be living, warned that the weather would be quite cold in December, and asked about our American community and where I had lived in the States.

MMS House in Imstenrade, Netherlands.

A roadside restaurant gave me my first taste of Dutch cuisine—a slab of cheese on a plain bun—and the guttural sounds of a strange tongue at nearby tables.

Back in the car the shifting time zones took their toll. I slept until we pulled into the driveway of the Medische Missiezusters (MMS) residence in the small village of Imstenrade that early December night. It would be my home for the next six weeks, with my orientation spilling over into the new year of 1970.

As in England, a roomful of older women rose to greet me when I entered the living room of the main house. After brief exchanges with the few who spoke English, one of them saw how tired I looked and escorted me to my bedroom.

The rectangular box that was to be my personal space held a rudimentary bed, desk, and chair—and that was enough. Fatigue wrapped me in its heavy arms. I had just enough energy to unpack and shower before collapsing into an exhausted sleep.

When the morning light nudged me awake, I resisted. *Couldn't I go back to sleep and discover this strange room was a dream?* But the insistent day stood at the foot of my bed with crossed arms, so I dressed and tracked the coffee scent to the kitchen, where I met the three young Filipinas assigned to the Pilot Project.

Cherubic Flora, a nutritionist, was as easy to talk to as her name was fun. Norma, a physician, appeared quite sophisticated, and Yoli, a pharmacist, looked like a feather she was so thin. They greeted me with warm smiles and welcomed me as their new companion. They also moaned over the cold European winter, so painful for their tropical bodies. When I said how overwhelmed I was feeling, they admitted they felt the same. We were all in our twenties, younger than the other sisters, and the only non-Dutch speakers.

At the communal lunch the blessing over the food was in Dutch, as were the ensuing conversations around me. I sat at one end of the long table, far from the other three, in awkward silence. After the meal many of the Dutch sisters greeted me, and I remembered them because they wore the same outfits as the night before. Some seemed more at ease than others, depending on how much English they knew. Others responded to what I said as though they understood me, but I suspected they didn't.

I would be guilty of that same guile in the coming days.

As that first day inched forward, I felt lost. Nothing was familiar. I longed to escape to my room for refuge from the struggle of listening to foreign sounds and trying to absorb so much new information. My attempts to speak the few Dutch words I was picking up felt fake, and I hesitated to say something wrong and sound stupid.

I recognized the danger of withdrawing from the discomfort that naturally arises in entering a foreign culture. Engaging with the other sisters and straining to listen to the language, even though it felt bewildering, was my task there, and I had to trust that it would help with the transition in Malawi.

Though Mass was a familiar ritual, I could only make out one or two words that sounded familiar in the Dutch liturgy in that first week. Yet the balm of the chapel and the daily time for quiet reflection and prayer soothed my disoriented spirit.

None of the Dutch sisters had been to America, so I was as strange to them as a newborn dropped on their front steps. Humor is such a connection between people, but my attempts at it often fell like a diver into an empty pool. I envied the three Filipinas, who could share their feelings in their mother tongue. Everyone but me had a private language in which to joke and share confidences. In the early days there, if Dutch or Tagalog conversations went on around me, I wondered if they were talking about me. That foolish reaction reflected my perception of myself as an outsider.

Once we had a day or two to find our way around the house and gain a sense of daily routines, we began the official introductory phase of the Pilot Project. Our six-week orientation was designed to prepare us to live with an all-Dutch MMS community in Malawi.

Each day we four gathered around a table for several classes: Dutch history, geography, politics, lifestyle, and culture. Some of the teachers and their presentations fascinated me, but one ancient grande dame of the community droned on and on and never invited discussion. The four of us fought to keep our eyes propped open.

I struggled most with the language classes. Linguistics and foreign languages had always been my weak points—someone once said my tongue was too thick—and the guttural Dutch pronunciations pressed my face into odd contortions as I tried to produce the requisite sounds. My efforts were a source of amusement to everyone else.

Fortunately, trips around the country broke up the relative tedium of sitting in class for hours. Over the following weeks the four of us, accompanied by a Dutch sister-guide, traveled to every corner of their small nation and met many Dutch people, from simple families to the heads of theology schools and hospitals. We visited the nearby Heerlen Children's Home for kids from broken families, as well as a department store in the city center where I felt like a child myself, unable to speak, disoriented by unintelligible signs and sounds.

To learn about the Dutch Catholic Church we spent an afternoon with the dean of the Tilburg Theological School and two young male theology students. Over coffee—and in English, thankfully—we explored our thoughts on Vatican II's call for engaging our humanity in the Church's work and living out the Christian message. We questioned Rome's hierarchical structure and celebrated the new respect for indigenous cultures. How striking that this group had so much in common. We were several nationalities all on the same wave length. Whatever one of us tried to express, in ever so halting a way, was understood by the others. Something transcended national boundaries and cultural patterns that day—a growing global consciousness.

On windmill platform.

One drive took us to a windmill where the owner invited us to climb to the circular platform at the top. High on the decking, I stood like the captain of a landlocked ship, looking out over the *polders*, the strips of land reclaimed from the sea. On other car trips around the Netherlands, bicyclists of every age pedaled alongside as we wended the narrow roads. I spied older men wearing *klompen*—the wooden shoes that I only knew as painted tourist booty.

Another day, arriving in Amsterdam, we headed straight for the Dam, the city's center. As we stood in the square, Dutch life swirled around us: skinny, clanging trams; the whirl of pedaled bicycles; and barges skimming the canal waters. A pause for photos doubled us over in laughter when three of the hundreds of pigeons landed on photographer Flora—one on her head, and one on each shoulder. She looked like one of the Dam's statues.

On the ride home from the city in a speeding train, Christmas lights flashed against the dark landscape, reminding me of the coming holiday. A deep blue homesickness seeped through my tired body.

The day before Christmas was a lonely time for me at Imstenrade. It was so subdued and quiet for Christmas Eve compared to the exciting bustle that would be going on in the US. After Vespers one of the sisters, who always seemed attuned to when we newcomers needed a boost, pulled out some sweets and found an English language station on her short-wave radio. We five lit candles and listened to the season's music while sharing how we celebrated Christmas as children. This link to past holidays satisfied a longing in me for something American, something of home.

At Midnight Mass in the flower-filled chapel, I contented myself with soaking up the atmosphere since I couldn't understand the sermon or the readings. Exiting after the service, greetings of *Zalick Kerstfest* (Merry

Christmas) flitted like swallows through the rooms. The brightly lit living room invited us to taste the holiday foods spread over several tables.

I had expected to stay up late to continue the celebration, but everyone retired early, so there was no one left to speak with. After a brief visit to the chapel, I went to my room where I wrote in my journal . . . and tried not to feel sorry for myself.

Most of my days since I left the States had been spent as a learner, which was surprisingly painful, rather than stimulating and mind-opening. I recognized in later years that competence has always been a core component of my identity, but in those days I was not feeling competent about anything. Although my interpersonal skills were well-honed, living in a different culture stripped me of the familiar cues that were my social parlance. Connecting to people through shared thoughts and feelings was essential to me, yet I was barely able to express more than greetings and the most superficial comments to Dutch-only speakers.

I became increasingly frustrated by my limited skills in language class, especially since my Filipina companions, who spoke several languages, showed more aptitude. I had reached a saturation point—all the words sounded the same. I even resented that Dutch children could speak with such ease when I couldn't.

One evening during that dark period, one of the younger Dutch sisters—a minority in that aging group—told me that she found it hard to live in that community because she wanted deeper communications with others. That helped me realize that my need to know and be known was at the heart of my language blues. It was a yearning for relationships and not just verbal skills.

When an American MMS stopped in Imstenrade for a few days of business, I shadowed her. Having someone around who had a sense of who I was and the culture that had shaped me was a solace. I choked up when it was time for her to leave. Now I was the only American again, which was to be my situation in Malawi. One of the Dutch sisters teased me: "Ah poor little one, now you are a solitary swimmer in the big Dutch sea."

But somewhere toward the end of those six weeks a turning point in my language assimilation occurred and I finally began to understand more. One evening a few of the Dutch sisters challenged me to Scrabble and I delighted them with my kindergarten vocabulary, sometimes even laying out a grownup word.

I knew my Dutch comprehension was improving when a sister came into the room to speak in private to my Dutch companion and begged, "Aimee please cover your ears. This is not for you to hear." Aha! She assumed that I would understand her Dutch. But as my linguistic abilities increased, my time in Imstenrade was evaporating, rushing to its conclusion just as I was feeling at home.

The four of us in the Pilot Project planned a party to thank the sisters for their hospitality. I ventured alone into the nearby Heerlen town center to shop for party items and get two injections I needed for Malawi. What a difference it was from my first visit to a department store six weeks earlier. I wanted to hug the sales clerks—they understood my Dutch.

The party that night began when Norma, Yoli, and Flora introduced the Philippines with graceful dances from the various islands. I helped with their performance of the *Tinikling*, in which dancers nimbly move their feet in and out of long bamboo poles clapped together on the floor to a three-point beat. Our audience, mostly large-boned, stocky women, were invited up to try the dance. To much laughter, all failed to escape the poles' attacks on their slow-moving ankles.

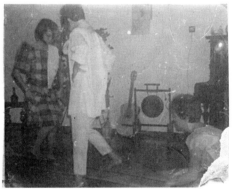

My contribution was a tour of the United States, drawing token costumes from a suitcase: a cowboy bandana, a sailor's cap, a straw farmer's hat, all accompanied by regional accents. I explained that our large family meant that my mom had to be resourceful and did much of her shopping in secondhand stores. I transformed myself with an old dress, oversized shoes, and a hat with a hole in it and sang "Secondhand Rose," one of my favorite songs.

Given my inability to carry a tune, I was stunned by a standing ovation and calls for an encore. As everyone was enjoying the food and drink after the show, I was mobbed by sisters who jokingly beseeched me for my autograph on their paper napkins.

The four of us ended the evening with a song and a litany of thanks. Afterwards as everyone was standing around, one of the sisters offered me a cigarette. Almost all the Dutch smoked—even nuns. The rising smoke got in my eyes, causing me to tear, as I wasn't used to smoking. I did it just to be social, using a proffered cigarette to somehow connect with the giver.

"Aimee, are you crying?" that sister asked, concern on her face.

"No, not really. It's just the smoke . . . " but I was crying on the inside, for I hated the thought of more good-byes.

In bed later that night, "Secondhand Rose" sang in my head. What a lovely emotion to know the sisters enjoyed my parting gift.

*

On Monday, January 12, 1970, our Pilot Project group disbanded, heading in different directions. Flora was going to Uganda first, Norma and Yoli to London, and I would leave soon for Germany—all of us enroute to Africa. I felt a twinge of sadness at our separation but knew it was short-lived. We were all to meet up in Nairobi in a few days and descend together on Malawi.

My last day in Imstenrade, in the midst of a final cleaning of my room, one of the middle-aged Dutch sisters popped her head in and slid herself onto my chair, obviously wanting to talk. A barrage of questions followed: "Aimee, how are you able to be so, so . . . happy? Our life as religious women is difficult and—how shall I say—sobering, but you . . . you seem not to be troubled by it all. Will religious life survive in this modern world? We are not getting any new candidates here in the Netherlands for our way of life. Is it dying? Is it very different in the Medical Mission communities in the States?"

The rush of questions overwhelmed me. I saw in her eyes and drooping mouth the pain behind them. I inched my way into answers, trying to tell her what was true for me: that it was our work that drew me on, and yes, living in community was challenging but also satisfying to me. Her face softened; her head nodded as I spoke.

When I didn't find more words waiting in the wings, I paused. "Was that what you wanted to know?"

Tears rimmed her eyelids. "Thank you. I've been struggling with my vocation for some time and needed to try to understand what allows you to be so full of life, when I feel so dead."

She quickly got up and left before I could respond.

Completing the last of my delayed packing, I was told that my American friend had arrived to take me to Germany. I ran through the house offering a hug with my *Tot ziens* (good-bye) to those sisters I could find and then returned for final embraces with those who gathered to wave me off. Though it was difficult to leave those women with whom I had finally forged a bond—the next stage called me on.

CHAPTER TWENTY-ONE

CHANGE IN PLANS

In Germany two sets of friends from the States generously escorted me around the cities of Bonn, Koblenz, and Heidelberg, traveling with the flow of the Rhine, Mosel, and Neckar Rivers. We toured a castle, a monastery, rural villages, and forested mountains. I wanted more time in that delicious landscape. The morsels of Germany whetted my appetite to return.

I never expected that my assignment to Malawi would allow me to visit so many places in transit. In those weeks in England and Europe I encountered a diversity of languages and world views, visited old friends in new settings, and nurtured my self confidence. I felt I had become a grownup and sophisticated traveler.

Awaking on what I thought was the last of my handful of days there, I ceremonially uncapped a medicine bottle and swallowed the first anti-malarial tablet, a reminder that all my travels so far were a prelude. That daily dose would become an ingrained habit in Africa. Taking my medicine reminded me that my days in Europe were over—or so I thought.

My planned itinerary began with a flight from Frankfurt to Rome, where I would join Norma and Yoli, who were arriving from London. After a two-hour layover, we three would fly overnight to Nairobi and connect with Flora, travelling from Uganda. Reunited, we would all travel to Malawi on African Air.

It was such a well-coordinated plan—until fog obscured the road to Frankfurt and became a soup near the airport. I could feel anxiety's tentacles twisting inside me. Arriving at my barely visible destination,

I bolted for the airport entrance—after a too-quick good-bye to my friend—and rushed to the Air Italia desk.

The agent confirmed my foreboding. "Sorry, but the planes are having trouble getting in and out. I doubt your flight will be leaving."

What would I do if I missed this flight? In that era before cell phones there was no way to contact Norma and Yoli. The only flight to Malawi from Nairobi was once a week! My worry index ratcheted up. If I missed that connecting flight in Nairobi, I would be trapped in Kenya for seven days—all alone. That felt scary. I didn't have enough money with me to last for a week anywhere . . .and how would I even get to Nairobi?

At midnight the Frankfurt airport closed down.

The agent advised me that I had only two options the next morning: Rome or Nairobi. Rome seemed the best choice since the Medical Mission Sisters' international headquarters was there. At least I could investigate getting to Malawi from a home base.

Since I didn't want to spend my meager money on a cab and hotel, I stayed overnight in the airport. Joining other detainees in the main terminal, I removed my sweaty boots, wrapped my coat around me, and wedged my handbag under my head. The barking of worries, the chill from lying on the metal bench, and a lumpy purse for a pillow kept the longed-for sleep at bay.

Roused by the fogless morning sun peering through the airport windows, I scurried to the terminal desk and booked the day's first flight to Rome. Shortly before noon Lufthansa Flight #10 lifted off from my Frankfurt "hotel," launching me into yet more unknowns.

CHAPTER TWENTY-TWO

ICING ON THE CAKE

Trying not to miss any sliver of Italy's beauty visible from the plane, I pressed my face to the tiny window, awed by the chisled Alps, whose jagged peaks gradually dissolved into the undulations of the blue Mediterranean.

After passing through customs, I knew to ask for help with the unfamiliar Italian phone. The answering voice at the Medical Mission Sisters Generalate assured me that someone would claim me shortly.

The drive through the Roman countryside to our headquarters was stunning: tropical flowers, top-heavy palm trees, and rows of cypress standing at attention. The southern sun began to thaw the northern chill lingering in my body from the Netherlands and Germany. We were driving past flat, farmed fields and grazing sheep when I caught my breath—the ancient city of Rome rose on the distant horizon like a queenly mirage.

A chorus of greetings and reaching arms embraced me when I entered the three-story institutional building. Though I didn't know most of them, I was relieved to be among my sisters again after feeling bereft when I missed my Frankfurt flight.

One of them informed me that Mother Anna Dengel, the foundress of Medical Mission Sisters, had asked to see me. *Could that be?* A short, sturdy woman with a warm, wrinkled face, Mother, then in her late sixties, was a revered figure in the Catholic world, and I was honored that she would make time for me.

MMS Generalate.

She was my spiritual mother and model, and I, a fledgling daughter in the religious community she had begun. I had spent brief times with her when she visited both Philadelphia and Washington, DC, but I was surprised that she remembered me among the hundreds of sisters who followed in her footsteps. What I thought would be a brief courtesy visit in her sitting room evolved into a warm, ninety-minute conversation. Mother was delighted that circumstances gave me the chance to see more of Rome and assured me the Generalate office would arrange my flight to Malawi. What a relief.

With a few days before my new departure date, I was free to explore the Holy City, the center of the Church's power and presence. What a whirlwind exposure to the wonders of this complex, ancient-yet-modern world. Each turn of a corner produced another stunning view: endless arches, monuments, temples, obelisks, and churches. I wandered the city agog, a child in a fairyland. It was the icing on the cake of my travels, not only because of its lucious beauty and warm climate, but also because it was an unexpected bonus. How could I be so blessed to experience several countries in Europe?

My days in Rome had the newness—the freshness—of a first kiss.

I can't forget my tour of the Catacombs, the vast underground burial site of the early Christians. As many as 50,000 martyrs' bodies or their  remnants rested in the unending rows of rough wall niches. As I stood in the dark, snaking tunnels where those who died for their faith were buried, I recalled my childhood fantasy of wanting to be a martyr—and the reality proved sobering.

On my last day Mother Dengel asked to see me again when I returned from touring the Vatican Museum on my own. We talked for another hour, but I grew increasingly anxious; I had to leave soon for my flight to Malawi and hadn't packed yet. Deciding to trust that it would all work out, I relaxed into my treasured time with that holy visionary.

It became clear as we talked that Mother found all the changes in religious life since Vatican II's recent decrees and the new directions of our 1967 Chapter painful to comprehend. She cried as she spoke of her concerns. I wanted to put my arms around that venerable woman, still wearing the habit that most of us had shorn, but hugging didn't feel appropriate. I tried to find comforting words. I spoke of the good things that had come with the changes, how it had freed all of us to give fuller expression to our religious commitment. It was evident, however, that her heart was burdened with new fears for the beloved community she had founded forty-four years earlier.

Looking back on that moment, I wish I had disregarded my caution and embraced her. So often in my life, my sense of what is "appropriate" has kept me from following my instincts, a choice I usually regret. Far more than sins of commission, omissions have left crumbs of remorse sprinkled on my life's path.

Our visit ended on a happy note though, and I promised I would write from Africa about the new Pilot Project endeavor, another of the many innovations she didn't understand. We finished just in time for me to race upstairs, pack, and sprint to the waiting car. Two sisters drove me to the airport and said a quick farewell as I leapt from the back seat. All my European departures were rushed, as I resisted tearing myself away until the last minute.

Darting through the terminal crowd to my gate, I reached it just as boarding started. *Phew!* I hardly had a minute to think about what was ahead . . . or what had happened in those three fly-by days in Rome and, even more, the precious gift of being in the presence of Mother Dengel.

That was the last time I would see her. When I had to leave Malawi, among my myriad emotions was a hope that Mother never found out what happened to me. I couldn't bear the thought of being a disappointment to her.

CHAPTER TWENTY-THREE

INTO AFRICA

An odd lot of people, mostly men, mingled at the gate for East African Airlines: British colonial types in jaunty hunting outfits, Indians in their long Sherwani jackets and pants, Africans in multicolored cotton fabrics. One of the few women, perhaps the sole American, I wore a simple pastel skirt, blouse, and lightweight jacket. Only the discreet silver cross suspended from a neck chain hinted that I was a nun.

Rome's bustle lay behind me; familiar faces were gone. My breath caught in my throat. I was a shiny-faced twenty-seven-year-old traveling alone to Africa.

My emotions clashed: excitement, anxiety, and uncertainty over what to expect on the remaining trip. After a short layover in Athens, I would leave the Western world and country-hop from Kenya to Tanzania and, finally, Malawi.

A young British sailor about my age sat beside me on the plane. To start a conversation I inquired about his destination. He puffed up and asserted that he was headed to Mombasa to join his ship. Digging into my "interesting facts" bag, I mentioned the only association I could find: "I read in an airport paper that the supply of rum allotted to Her Majesty's sailors is being decreased. Had you heard that?" A momentary pained look flashed across his face . . . and then we both laughed.

We connected easily and I bombarded him with questions about his life.

"How long have you been a sailor? Is it your first time to Mombasa? . . . It sounds so exotic. What does your training involve? What will you be doing on board the ship?" Focusing on him waylaid my own anxiety. After answering all my questions he shifted uncomfortably in his seat.

"So, uh . . . Missus, what'll yah be doin' on this plane to Africa?"

"I'm going to Malawi. I'm a Catholic nun and my community has a hospital there where I'll work as a nurse."

"So, uh . . . How long'll yah be stayin'?"

"Well . . . I don't know. In the past our sisters would work in the missions for most of their lives or until they got sick and had to return home. But many things have been changing in my religious community and the intent is to bring sisters back for renewal every seven years."

"Blimey," he uttered, his brow furrowed. The fact of being away from home that long silenced him; perhaps the life of a nun seemed a foreign land he didn't know how to enter.

Our chatter drifted off after that. We both napped fitfully during the five-hour flight to Nairobi until roused by the stewardess with an offer of coffee.

While I ate breakfast, the early light out the window was pulling back the covers from a sleeping Kenya below. As the plane droned downward, only a dense carpet of trees interspersed with circular brown huts was visible.

Where were the cities, the buildings? Oh my God! The naked reality of the continent struck like a sledgehammer.

Several African men sat along the grassy edge of the landing strip and pointed at our plane as it touched down and taxied along the rough runway. *What were they doing there? It wasn't safe to be so close to a landing plane!* It was extraordinary to me that this could happen at an airport.

The captain announced a forty-five-minute layover, but I didn't want to exit the plane. My stomach heaved. Fear of what was outside glued me to my seat until workers spilled into the plane to clean it, scooting me out. The time had come.

This was not Europe!

Africans in layered fabrics and robes awash in color dominated the terminal. In the slow-moving crowd, Europeans, looking fresh from safari—khaki shirts and pants with uncountable pockets—merged with swarthy Indians, the merchant class of Africa. Alien sounds, the stink of bodies in the tropical heat, and the gruesome sight of animal skins, claws, and ivory tusks hanging in the shops all seemed . . . primitive. The assault on my senses unnerved me.

Spying a sign for the women's washroom, I ducked inside, needing a private place to hide. When I returned to the waiting area, a well-dressed young African smiled and introduced himself.

"Hello, Madam. You seem distressed. I live here in Kenya. Can I be of service?" He had noticed the raw fear on my face.

"Thank you, but no. I'm on my way to Malawi. I've never been in Africa before, so I'm a bit overwhelmed."

"Do not worry, Madam. We Africans are very kind, and we will help you find your way." I thanked him for his supportive words. We spoke for a few minutes before it was time for me to return to the plane's womb-like security.

Flying next into Tanzania's airport, I spied the sinuous Zanzibar archipelago just off the lip of the continent. It triggered a desire to escape to some private island—any place other than my destination. I craved a setting that wouldn't require anything from me—only a walk on the beach, a swim in warm waters. The fantasy served as an antidote to my mounting anxiety.

But no island awaited, only another airport—Dar es Salaam.

Drained by my reaction to the sights in Nairobi, I hunkered down in my seat to gather my inner resources for the next and final stop just two hours away—Blantyre, Malawi. Fortunately, no one shooed me out of the plane this time.

On the last leg of my journey, Lake Malawi, one of the ten largest lakes in the world and part of the Great Rift Valley, filled most of the landscape below until it gave way to a blur of green treetops and ribbons of brown roads weaving through the dense bush.

Further south, humped mountains, like packs of camels, loomed on the horizon. Massive cumulus clouds nuzzled the peaks of those prehistoric ranges. As the plane started its descent into Chileka airport, scattered thatched roofs came into view.

Still no sign of civilization as I knew it.

Our plane was the only one in sight when I disembarked, my bags weighing down my shoulders, my heart pushing up against my throat. In seconds, I was sweating profusely from the sun's scorching heat reflected back from the cement runway.

The crowd drifted toward the terminal, a long, two-storied structure with a corrugated metal roof. People of every skin shade, from deep black to bland white, shouted and waved as they leaned over the airport balcony ahead. Searching the rambunctious crowd, I prayed, *Please God, let someone be here.* I hoped the sisters in Rome remembered to contact Phalombe to claim me.

A deep sigh escaped my tight chest when two women wearing white uniforms and small head scarves eagerly beckoned me. I was easy to spot, the only unaccompanied female in the queue at the terminal entrance.

Entering the low building with the hand-painted sign "Chileka Airport," a crew of Africans jostled me as they carted the luggage from the plane to the customs table. The acrid scent of their bodies made me want to plug my nose. Flies and other unknown bugs filled the air and crawled over every surface. In a small, dilapidated room, two men in pressed khaki shorts and shirts and red berets stood behind a wooden table. Upright and unsmiling, officious in their bearing, they were the customs officers. Bags had been thrown onto the table, and I pointed out mine to one official, who promptly handed them to me. With a quick snap of his hand the second serious man stamped my passport, leaving another ink bruise on its pages. My momentous arrival in Malawi was just another day's work for them, and I, just another white face.

Exiting through the gate to the outside, I almost jumped into the arms of the two sisters. It was a delightful surprise to be met by an American I knew from the States, though she informed me she was leaving Malawi the next day. She introduced me to Sister Miriam, a blond Dutch woman in her forties, the coordinator of the Malawi Pilot Project. I liked her immediately.

*

Almost two months had passed since I left Philadelphia and traveled through England, the Netherlands, Germany, and Italy—all such worldly experiences for the provincial young girl I was.

Now at last, my destiny would take wing. A few hours away waited my new Dutch community and the place where I would live and work with Malawians. Not until I reached Phalombe would I finally learn the specifics of the Cultural Orientation Program Experiment (COPE), referred to as the Pilot Project. I was a willing guinea pig in that nine-month exploratory program about which I knew so little except for studying the Malawian language and culture and living with our Dutch sisters. Though going into it somewhat blindly, my heart and mind were wide open to whatever would be required of me. I had great expectations.

The first part of my journey was over. My next—and biggest—challenge was about to begin. I didn't know how long I would stay in Malawi, though I hoped it would be for many years. Since I had been a well-regarded Medical Mission Sister with leadership responsibilities in my American community, I assumed that would continue.

I was unprepared for what was to come.

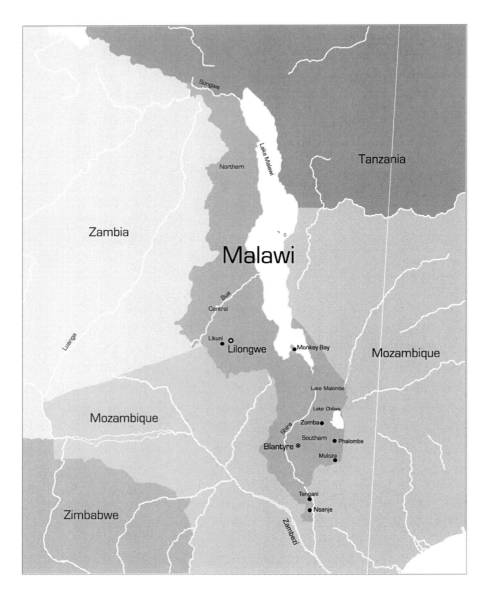

CHAPTER TWENTY-FOUR

NATIONAL GEOGRAPHIC

After jamming in my luggage, we piled into the car for the nine-mile drive to Blantyre on our way to my new home in Phalombe. The sisters told me that Norma, Yoli, and Flora had already arrived from Europe without any delays, so I was the last to show up, several days late. They offered a preview of what to expect at the Phalombe compound: its isolated setting at the foot of the Mulanje Mountains, the layout of the hospital and our living quarters, and some of the sisters I would soon be meeting. Fatigue and overload prevented me from holding up my end of the conversation, so I was grateful for their easy chatter.

Throughout the ride I stared wide-eyed at the alien landscape unrolling like a carpet around me. Malawi was a National Geographic magazine come alive—but with me inside it.

We drove slowly past dusty, earth-colored women walking barefoot along the side of the road with immense bundles of kindling or a single hoe balanced on their heads. Babies were tethered to their backs with the same colorful fabrics worn as a skirt or sarong. Their clothes were tattered and soiled; the sleeves of Western-style blouses hung by a few scant threads from their shoulder seams.

Barefoot children dressed in rags ran alongside our car with noisy shouts and flapping arms. Other children stood and stared from the roadside, their bulging bellies the telltale sign of malnutrition.

Wiry, worn men riding rickety bicycles pedaled slowly against the heat. Thatched roofs hung like untrimmed hair over rectangular mud walls while skeletal cows wandered in nearby grasses.

Malawi's ranking as the nation with the second-lowest per capita income in the world—forty-five dollars a year—was evident everywhere I looked.

Many sections of Blantyre, the southern region's capital, looked like an old Wild West town. While there were a few modern structures, many were single-story, rudimentary buildings constructed of wood or locally made brick. Milling crowds of people laden with baskets or bags filled the road we drove down; puny dogs slunk around the outskirts. Ours was one of the few cars in sight.

Sister Miriam informed me that Blantyre was named after the Scottish birth town of the famed local explorer David Livingstone. Though it didn't look impressive, it was the commercial capital and one of the oldest towns in that very underdeveloped country.

We stopped to meet the district superior of Medical Mission Sisters in Malawi, a middle-aged Dutch woman with a dour expression. Her words of welcome were restrained, and I was too tired to do more than rally a brief smile. That first encounter with the woman who would be my highest superior in the country left me ill at ease.

After dropping off the American sister in Blantyre, our next stop was the neighboring town of Limbe to buy meat at one of the Indian-owned general stores. It was a crudely framed structure covered by an overhanging tin roof and supported by hand-hewn posts. A rusted Fanta soda sign dangled over the store entrance.

While sister made her purchase inside, I gawked at the pulsating life beyond the car window. One woman tied her baby onto her back, slipped off high-heel shoes—perhaps worn to  go shopping in town—and headed down a dirt road. She joined a long line of swaying bodies carrying their wares home on their heads. Farther on when we stopped to get petrol, four men jumped up to clean the car's windows, hoping for some coins.

I was completely unprepared for the sights assaulting my tired eyes and overwhelmed brain. The images of poverty and hardship hit me with a one-two punch.

From Limbe we started the two-hour ride to Phalombe along roads that changed from poorly paved, to rutted, to pockmarked with deep holes. We had to dodge rocks as though we were inside a pinball machine. My mind slid deeper into shock with each passing mile, while my body banged and bumped inside the car, leaving bruises on my skin.

Gradually the mountains around Blantyre merged into flat plains and rain came, turning the dirt roads to mud and forcing the villagers to huddle under thatched roofs. I had arrived in Malawi during *dzinja,* the rainy season, when thunderstorms rolled in each midday for months.

We were less than an hour from Phalombe when the Mulanje Mountains rose like a fortress on the horizon, soaring ten thousand feet high. Waterfalls cascaded from the halo of clouds loitering on the peaks. The late afternoon sun splashed the sky's colors onto their vertical slopes. A rainbow crowned the range. *Had we come upon a scene from South Pacific? Perhaps Bali Hai?*

Nearing my new home, we drove past Likulezi Catechetical Training Center, where I would soon attend a three-month course in Malawian language and culture, the first component in the nine-month Pilot Project ahead.

A few minutes later we reached the home and hospital of Medical Mission Sisters, nestled in a crook of the mountains in the middle of nowhere. We turned in at the sign *Chipatala Cha Banja Loyera* (Holy Family Hospital), bumped along a smaller dirt road winding though the property, and pulled up to a simple, one-story cinderblock building, the main living quarters of the sisters. Some of them had gathered for their afternoon tea ritual and were there to greet me.

My exhaustion was so great, no memory of the rest of that day remains except for the juicy pineapple slices we had for dessert. After supper one of the sisters showed me the path to my room in the house I would share with five Dutch sisters. The other three Pilot Project members were in the main residence, so I was the only newcomer in the house on the fringe of the compound. The ten-minute walk took me past several sheds, vegetable gardens, the hospital, nursing school, and through a densely wooded area before reaching my new living quarters.

My bedroom had two catty-corner windows—one looking out over the front porch and the path I would walk several times a day to reach the main buildings on the property. The other looked toward the few mud brick homes of the local house staff, about ten yards away.

I intended to unpack but fell into the bed with my clothes still on, remembering to pull the mosquito net around me. I fell asleep easily, lulled by the night sounds of unknown creatures outside my room.

The next day I sketched a map of the compound to send to my family.

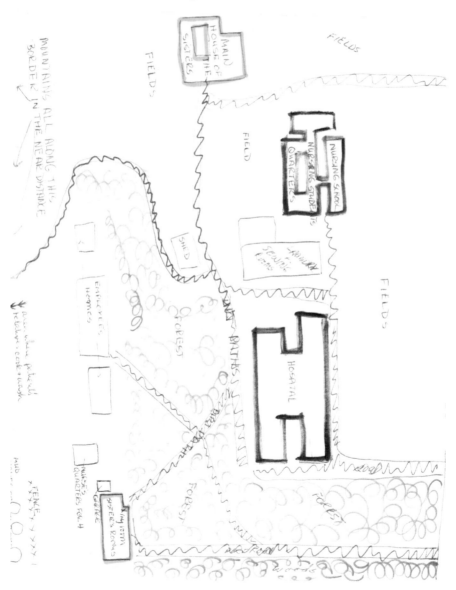

PHALOMBE COMPOUND

CHAPTER TWENTY-FIVE

NOTES UNDER A MOSQUITO NET

Arooster's crow at first light and the sounds of crying children and strange voices drew me from deep sleep. I wanted to hide under the sheet but forced myself to get up and ready for what the day might hold.

On the muddy path through the woods and alongside the hospital, I came upon a Malawian couple with a young child. Having practiced the basic greetings *Moni* (Hello) and *Muli bwangi* (How are you?), I felt proud to greet them in the national language of Chichewa—but assumed I butchered those few words when they clapped their hands and doubled over laughing. My confidence melted—my first linguistic attempt was a failure.

In later weeks I understood they were simply delighted by my efforts. I experienced the ready laughter of Malawians as warm and friendly—an invitation to relationship. There is good reason why Malawi is called "The Warm Heart of Africa."

Reaching the main building at the end of my walk across the compound, I found the kitchen and got some coffee. Since no one was in sight, I undertook a brief tour on my own. The sisters' living area was a one-story, U-shape building with an interior green lawn housing about sixteen bedrooms along two sides. The living and dining room, chapel, and kitchen were clustered at the front.

After a simple bread-and-cheese lunch in the afternoon and subdued conversations with the rest of the community, I returned to my bedroom intending to unpack the luggage still scattered over the floor, but fatigue pushed me into bed. After a death-like sleep I woke in time to cross the compound once again for Mass and supper. During the evening meal, flies blitzed the room and crawled on everything. The main dish was goat, each mouthful yielding more gristle and bony nuggets than meat. Between the flies and the goat, I was on the brink of nausea.

Everyone then migrated to the living room to socialize for the remainder of the evening. Many of the sisters smoked, as in the Netherlands community in Imstenrade. It seemed a common European pleasure. Those who spoke better English approached me. I tried to be cordial in spite of my persistent exhaustion and sense of dislocation, even disembodiment. I left the group early to get still more sleep. A comment that three of the sisters had malaria over the last few days stayed with me, so I carefully tucked my mosquito net around my bed frame before writing in my journal:

> I am in a state of shock. It really scares me. I am so overwhelmed by the primitiveness of the landscape, the isolation created by the surrounding wall of mountains, the heat and bugs, the poverty— everything. I can't imagine a future for myself here. I am a displaced person; my body is here, but it's not connected to me. I'm having negative reactions to everything, in spite of my naturally positive personality and finally reaching my long desired destination. I feel so disconnected. I must remember to be patient, must not project my present feelings into the future.

Two days passed in that mental state before I started feeling more like myself. It helped when Sister Miriam spent the following few days orienting us four newcomers to the compound.

The hospital, our first stop, was another one-story, H-shaped structure with a tin-roofed verandah running along all sides. It consisted of separate, dormitory-style wards for men, women, children, and expectant mothers, as well as a small operating room with sparse equipment, an outpatient department, a dispensary, and an x-ray darkroom. The windows and doors had no screens, providing free access to insects. It felt shabby and alarmingly rudimentary. The wards were bare of all but rusting iron beds, grass-stuffed mattresses, and patients. There were none of the usual medical accoutrements found in a patient's room in America. People sat or slept on the dusty cement floor alongside their ill relatives.

Since there was no kitchen, the women prepared food at a nearby shelter nestled in a grove of trees behind the house where I slept. The *chitondo* was a wide open space covered with a thatched roof where women cooked over fires and washed the clothes of  their sick family members. They slept there at night, as they usually came from far away.

People constantly wandered through the hospital and surrounding yard, bringing in food from the *chitondo* or sitting on the floor of the hospital verandah in small groups, chatting and playing with their children.

*

I continued to spill my reactions to what I was seeing and learning onto my journal pages:

> Today, I forced back tears as I looked into the faces of all those sick patients who lacked even the most basic comforts. Sister Miriam told us about the range of conditions they treat here: difficult deliveries because of the heavy weights on a mother's back, machete wounds, malaria, bilharzia, tropical ulcers, hookworm, anemia, tuberculosis, to name a few. The burns are awful to see—especially on children who too often fall into open cooking fires.

She said that there are 200,000 people for every doctor in this country. At present, only one sister-doctor works here. I'm going to have to learn an entirely new way of practicing nursing. I hardly know anything about these conditions or how to practice in this destitute environment.

The hospital was so barren and dirty. I felt the impulse to just start cleaning it. I think that the sisters should do more to improve the appearance, but maybe there's a reason why it's like this. Of course, I really don't know enough to judge yet.

Meeting the Malawian nurses and other staff was a joy, though it was hard to keep their unfamiliar African names in my head. The young nursing students giggled as we greeted them, speaking hesitant English, just as I will when I begin their language.

We walked a short distance to the laundry shed, which served both the hospital and the sisters—at least those who risked their clothes to the

system. It consisted of a large, tin-roofed structure with big tubs of water heated by fires underneath. The workers cleaned the items by pounding them on massive rocks on the shed floor, then hung everything on outside lines. Sudden storms arrived every day in the rainy season, soaking the drying items. If things needed to be ironed, the workers used a heavy coal-filled iron . . . made of iron.

Then on to the fields and gardens, which appeared wildly overgrown. Some hired men were cutting down the grasses with their machetes, large cleaver-style knives used for countless daily functions. Others were sweeping the dirt pathways with sticks tied together like a broom, watching for snakes as they worked.

Exhausted that night from all the new and strange sights and information, I crashed into sleep. It had been a full day of introductions to my new home. The following morning we would tour more of the compound. Fortunately, we were being exposed to things gradually, as I was only able to absorb a little at a time. It all still felt overwhelming.

After Mass and breakfast we visited the nursing school and their living quarters. About fifty young African girls attended the school, most of them coming from villages where they had no exposure to Western ways. It was true culture shock for them—and I could empathize.

They first had to learn basic hygiene: how to wash themselves at sinks, use toilets, and launder their uniforms. They spent three years in the program: two in regular nursing, and a third year of midwifery. The program, taught in English, was a demanding curriculum from the ground up.

The four of us in the Pilot Project were not the only new arrivals at Phalombe. The new class of students had just come, so we were invited to attend their welcoming ceremony that evening. After talks by the teaching sisters and greetings from the senior students, the girls turned on an ancient record player and began to dance to sixties music. Unable to just watch, Flora and I jumped up and joined them. I had always loved to dance as a teen and thought it was a way to connect with these young student nurses.

I'm not sure the older Dutch sisters in the room approved. Yet the evening's blemish came not from their possible disapproval, but from my own feelings of competitiveness and insecurity as revealed in my journal:

It was evident at the party tonight that Norma, Yoli, and Flora are more facile than I at attempting to speak Chichewa with the girls. I feel threatened by this, the sense that I'm not as socially at ease as they. Am I being competitive, wanting to be the best at this new

*experience, or is it revealing my own insecurity? It
seems that I do better when I am alone with the Dutch
or Malawians, but with the other three newcomers,
if they appear more capable and competent in any
situation, I withdraw into myself.*

This tendency to compare myself to my companions, especially in language fluency, hounded me throughout the coming months. I failed to account for the fact that they already spoke several languages while I was a mono-linguist, struggling with Chichewa as I had struggled with the Dutch language.

The trickery of any new language became apparent to me a few weeks later when I traveled with two of the sister-nurses to a few outlying clinics connected with our hospital. I tried to practice my limited Chichewa with the Malawians—to the amusement of all. At one of the feeding stations, I was helping to distribute containers of dry milk for the babies and asked the moms to give me their small carrying cloths to take home the *mpaka* (cat) rather than the intended word, *mkaka* (milk).

While I didn't mind being laughed at—and laugh everyone did—my confidence and competency in both Dutch and Chichewa was repeatedly eroded by confusing experiences and miscommunications that chewed on my ego, leaving me emotionally frayed and ragged.

How could I succeed in the Pilot Project, in living in Malawi, if I couldn't understand and speak with the people?

CHAPTER TWENTY-SIX

PHALOMBE LOCALES

Within walking distance from our compound stood the Phalombe Catholic Church, a dark-stone edifice with three sky-piercing steeples—its architecture belonging more in Europe than tropical Malawi. The inside of the church, a vaulted, empty space with a simple wooden altar at the far end, held no pews or chairs other than a few crude stools. The people offered them to us when we attended our first Mass there as part of our orientation to the local Catholic community. We typically celebrated daily Mass in our own little chapel.

I wondered if the people gave us the stools out of deference to the *azungu* (white foreigners) or because we were nuns? The Dutch sisters in our small group sat on them; I chose to join the women on the cement floor. I wasn't sure what others thought about that. Was I breaking some code of behavior in the eyes of the sisters or the Malawians? I did what seemed natural to me, but I needed to learn what was expected in that cultural setting.

The men sat on the floor on the left side of the church and wore pants and shirts. On the other side, the women were dressed in riotous combinations of colors and fabrics. Many of the mothers nursed their little ones during the service, their breasts comfortably exposed. One chubby child, after suckling from his mother, waddled over to another woman who let him plop in her lap.

During the Chichewa Mass two women came down the aisle balancing pitchers of water and wine on their heads and handed the jugs to the priest. The congregation sang their responses in loud, repetitive chants. At the consecration of the hosts, they clapped their hands in rhythm. The cadence of it all made me want to move my body, get up and dance to the beat—and maybe shoo away some flies at the same time.

Scads of flies filled the humid space, enough for each of us to have our own coterie of attentive insects. The sensation of several crawling on my legs and arms made my hairs stand on end—I spent most of the service discreetly trying to swat them away. I noticed, however, that most of the congregants ignored them, resigned to their persistent presence. *Would I learn how to do that?* Between the music and the flies, it was hard for me to maintain a nun-like decorum.

As we filed out into the bright morning sun afterwards, I kept repeating *Moni* to the people who swirled around me. Though that was all I could say, I hoped to show by my smiles and handshakes how much I wanted to connect with them. I also enjoyed making funny faces at the children, who shyly smiled or laughed back. I couldn't wait for the language course to start. I hated feeling so mute with those friendly neighbors.

*

Continuing our cultural introduction the next day, Sister Miriam took the four of us to Phalombe Primary School, a ten-minute walk from our compound. Those young ones were the fortunate few receiving formal education. Most children in the country at that time had no schooling. The rudimentary mud-brick schoolhouse held eight standards (grades). The four lower classes were taught in Chichewa; the four upper levels were taught in English. The children had to share the few rough seats and desks or sit on the ground. Papers, pencils, and books were notably missing from the scene; the teacher and a scratched blackboard appeared to be the only resources for their learning.

The seventh standard teacher, a warm and well-spoken young woman, invited us to see their gardens, part of their agricultural studies. The majority of the students would do subsistence farming of maize and ground nuts after finishing school. Most Malawians grew barely enough to feed their own families; if there was extra, it was sold in the local market.

Each eager boy and girl tried to get our attention, proudly pointing out his or her growing plants as we wandered through the fields. After we had surveyed the entire area, the teacher called the children together in a circle. "Do you want to ask our guests anything?"

I expected a shy silence from the children, but we were deluged with questions. "How much maize do you grow? Do you use plows or hoes? Do you make ridges when you plant?"

I was taken aback. Other than my farm obedience at the motherhouse as a young novice, I had no idea of growing anything other than house plants. I tried to explain that only certain people in America, called farmers, grew crops. Everyone else bought their food from a store. The students shook their heads—either in pity or disbelief.

The class broke into smaller groups; some boys gravitated toward me when they learned I was from America. They asked about our very tall buildings (skyscrapers): "What is inside them?"

"Well, people live in them or have offices in them where they go to work every day." They then questioned how those people get from the bottom to the top. "Well," I started, "there are these little rooms inside the building that go up and down by pulleys...umm, pulleys are these metal cables... umm...with heavy weights...." I was in over my head trying to explain elevator engineering to kids living in mud and grass huts.

*

Another day's adventure began when the local superior invited me to see the Phalombe market on the way to visiting one of our hospital staff. The two *kobedi* (pennies) entrance fee allowed us into the market where scores of dusty bodies milled around a flat, treeless field. They gawked at us, the only white faces in the crowd. Large sheets of fabric or plastic spread on the ground were piled with fruits, vegetables, and tobacco. One vendor displayed a goat's head, raw chunks of unknown meat, and intestines—all used as a landing base for flies. I was doing my own gawking.

A group of children followed us as we tiptoed among the colorful, and at moments, odiferous items scattered everywhere. One poor child lay on a patch of grass, clearly sick and feverish. We searched for his family, but so many in the crowd looked sick: eye discharges, runny noses, coughs, distended bellies. Flies covered the eyes of infants carried on the backs of mothers who couldn't see behind to swat them away, if they even would.

I said *Moni* to everyone, shook hands without regard for cleanliness, and studied all the food items with an admixture of interest and revulsion.

Afterwards, the superior and I walked to the nearby village to visit Dyson, one of our cooks. We were such a novelty that people poured out from their huts to see us. The crowd grew to at least forty people, most of them curious kids. I plowed through a prickly maize field with a little girl attached to each hand, one with the sparse, reddish hair of a malnourished child, the other wearing only a piece of worn rag beneath her bulging belly.

Dyson's chest expanded when we reached his hut and he greeted us as though we were dignitaries. After a brief visit with him and his family, we left with a gift of one squawking chicken and two pumpkins. Ever since my days on the farm at the Philadelphia motherhouse, I couldn't stand live chickens. I begged my companion to carry it, while I lugged the pumpkins.

As she and I were settling in the truck to leave, an older man left a crowd of people enjoying *mowa* (homemade beer) and came up to the driver's side window. He was clearly drunk and spoke to her while pointing at me. She started laughing, then translated for me. "He wants to marry you. I am to leave you right over there," she said, pointing to a wooded area, "so he can carry you off." He continued to plead, hoping to sway her, but she felt it wasn't a good match.

CHAPTER TWENTY-SEVEN

WHEN THE RAINS CAME

I was only in Phalombe for about a week when the sister administrator, one tough woman, informed me after breakfast that I had to learn how to drive all the mission's vehicles: a Volkswagen beetle, a pickup truck, and a creaky ambulance well into old age. Since they were all stick shift, I had another new skill to learn. I had only driven automatic transmission cars in the States. Once I mastered the VW, I would graduate to the pickup truck, then the ambulance.

Sinas, one of our house staff and the only trusted Malawian driver, was assigned to teach me. Since his English and my Chichewa were equally limited, I wasn't sure how the lessons would go. He began my lesson by driving around the compound to demonstrate the three pedals and the gear shift. Starting—stopping—forward—backward. Then it was my turn at the controls—a switch of drivers that came much too soon. *Grind . . . jerk . . . grind . . . jerk*. Grimace.

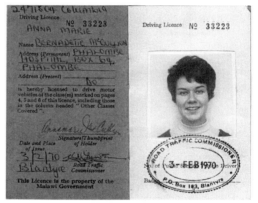

Malawian driver's license.

Each time I was supposed to change gears, Sinas reached over, grabbed my calf and moved it from the gas pedal to the clutch. When he first touched my bare leg, I was shocked. *Was he being fresh? Taking advantage of my newness in the seclusion of the car?* A look at his earnest face assured me that he was simply trying to demonstrate the timing of my footwork on the pedals since he didn't own the needed vocabulary.

Several sweaty hours were consumed in learning all three vehicles and their idiosyncrasies over the next few days of lessons. But even the best teacher and repeated practice behind the wheel failed to prepare me for driving in the rainy season.

About a month after my arrival and still a neophyte in the driver's seat, I drove to Blantyre with another sister. We had to shop for household items and rabies vaccine the hospital needed; so many people had been bitten by dogs recently. I was nervous about the two-hour drive into town, especially since it was the rainy season. The roads I would have to drive on, difficult to maneuver even in the dry season, were reported to be very bad.

Shortly into the trip we reached the first stream we had to traverse. Water was already lapping over the rough wooden bridge, but there was minimal current. I managed the crossing, though the water reached up to the top of the tires.

At the Tuchila River, water cascading down the mountain created a rushing torrent over that more flimsy bridge. We sat for an hour on one side of the river hoping that the level would drop so we could safely cross. I became increasingly impatient, knowing how much we had to do in town and wanting to get back before dark, given the dangerous roads. About a foot of angry water on the bridge remained, but I decided to chance it and forded the still-rushing water. Prayers of gratitude spilled from my lips when we made it to the other side without being swept away.

We slipped and slid for the remainder of the ride to town and back. My heart was in my mouth the entire trip. I had sweated so much I had to change my soaked clothes when I reached home.

But the rainy season affected more than travel.

With the rains came the insects. Consumed with mating, thousands of flying ants rose from the ground each day. At mealtimes, the dining room felt like a cow barn.

One evening I returned to my room after supper to find that the rarely-used electric ceiling bulb had switched on when the hospital generator was used for an earlier emergency surgery. The bulb's light had attracted hundreds of flying ants into my room. They swarmed over the walls, my bed, and desk, landing on me as I came in. Brushing them off my body, I ran into the hall closet for an insect bomb to spray my room. After waiting for it to work, I returned to witness the carnage and sweep up their tiny carcasses. It was a good thing bugs didn't bother me, since insects took every opportunity to share my living space.

One morning after washing a blouse and laying it to dry over the edge of my bed, I came back later to discover a conga-line of ants zig-zagging along the floor to the small puddle of water from my dripping top. I stomped them to death or drowned the remnants when I rewashed my ant-covered blouse. I hated killing all those insects, but I was kinder to the colorful lizards that lounged or wiggled across my bedroom walls and scurried across the floor every day. I considered them amusing roommates and often talked to them.

Snakes, however, scared me, especially the poisonous ones, which were everywhere in the bush. A few days after my arrival I heard that some of the boys from the nearby houses had chased a deadly black mamba into the tree next to my bedroom window. The men used their machetes to cut the grasses around its base to better see the snake when it came down.

Since I didn't know if it had been caught, I was anxious going up to my room that night in the dark. I kept looking up toward the tree and then raking the dirt path ahead with my flashlight in search of its long body. I let out several deep sighs when I was safely inside the house. I never saw or heard anything further about that snake, though I had many other snake sightings during my time in Malawi.

But I had one frightening experience that haunted me much more than the snakes. The Mulanje hyenas living in the nearby mountains are the only hyenas known to attack humans. They usually moved down and away from the mountain when the locals were burning off the slopes. We were advised to be careful, as they were recently clearing parts of the bush not far from our compound. Often after dark, I would hear the hyenas' distant howling, a sinister sound like the devil laughing.

Not feeling well one evening, I left the main building after dinner to walk the ten minutes to my house. I hadn't thought to tell anyone I was leaving. The compound was black as pitch since the generator was off, as usual. Flashlight in hand to guide my steps on the dirt path, I passed by the gardens, the laundry shed, and the hospital before entering the

stretch of forest between the main compound and my house. Halfway into the woods I heard the unmistakable sound of a hyena in the bush to my right. Turning toward the sound, I caught a glint of steely eyes. I froze. I was alone. *Should I try to run for my house, still more than fifty yards ahead? Run back to our main building? To the hospital?* While panic pummeled my brain, my legs kept walking a measured pace, fearing that any quick movement might provoke the possibly hungry creature. Though it was a cool night, sweat prickled my scalp and dripped down my back. I moved forward, one foot after the other, staring straight ahead, afraid to look back and see the hyena following me. I slowly gained the edge of the house—catapulted onto the verandah—and fell through the door.

My chest was about to burst as I tried to catch my breath. Sobs came.

During the night, I was awakened by a hyena's cadenced moaning outside my window, possibly warning that he was still waiting for me.

CHAPTER TWENTY-EIGHT

TWO DIFFERENT WORLDS

Malawi in the early 1970s was a human sea of four million dark-skinned Africans with a smattering of about one thousand expatriates. That ratio didn't discomfort me, but I was bothered when it appeared that my white skin gave me undeserved status.

On one of our many early Pilot Project excursions, Sister Miriam and the four of us newcomers had gone to a nearby village to witness a celebration for President Kamuzu Banda. While we were moving along the outskirts of the huge excited crowd, an official-looking young man in a crisp shirt and tailored slacks approached and beckoned us to follow him. Our formal escort brought us to sit in the grandstand with village chiefs and government dignitaries.

While I appreciated the kindness, I saw no reason for us to be favored. The four of us had just arrived in the country and hadn't done anything to deserve the elevated view of the festivities. It occurred to me later that perhaps the gesture was their way of recognizing the work of the sisters at our hospital and had less to do with our white skin or us as individuals. But I never knew for sure.

As my interactions with local Malawians unfolded over the days and weeks, my respect and appreciation of them deepened. These kind people were always ready to give a smiling *Moni*.

No one was a stranger. They seemed to laugh at life—though I felt they had every reason to cry, given their lack of the most basic necessities, let alone comforts.

As the realization sank in that I was living among people whose ancestors had been ripped away—like trees uprooted from the earth—and taken into slavery, tears filled my heart. Racism had offended me since childhood. Now I was in Africa, the ancestral homeland of African-Americans, rubbing shoulders and shaking hands with people like those who were carried off in shackles, torn from their families, their villages, their world.

Slave trade was introduced in Malawi by the Swahili-Arab traders in the nineteenth century, and slave markets were established at different points in Malawi, one being Phalombe. Humans were auctioned and sold to different parts of the world at the East Africa markets. Some slave trade routes controlled by Yao chiefs passed through the Mulanje Mountains in Phalombe District. Two other Yao chiefs terrorized the tribes of the Lower Shire Plain.

The history of slavery in the areas of Malawi where I would later work confronted me with the truth that I walked on ground that had witnessed horrific human suffering—a suffering that continues there today under modern forms of political, economic, and environmental slavery.

I was deeply moved by the repeated realization that these people had the same basic concerns as my mom and dad: the care of their families, shelter and food, work, weather, neighbors. Yet their struggles to survive were far more life-draining than back home.

My journal entry held my reflections on my evolving grasp of what I was learning:

> When I think about what this time in Africa means
> for me, it is an opportunity to discern "having" from
> "being." To strip down to the essentials of life in a
> personal confrontation—to be stunned into elemental

living. My American consciousness has been dulled by materialism; the Malawians have not yet had theirs fully awakened. They need MORE to be more; I need LESS to be more.

As I interacted with the staff and nursing students at our hospital, I felt they accepted and liked me. Malawians I met in my travels responded to my obvious efforts to meet them as individuals—and I was an ongoing source of amusement to the lively children who recognized how much I enjoyed playing and teasing them. They swarmed like bees wherever I went and the teasing was mutual.

One afternoon after talking with the kids next door, I left them to walk to the hospital. When I heard loud giggling, I turned quickly to see they had all followed me and that Dorothea, a petite six-year-old, was mimicking the way I walked, to the delight of the others. We all laughed and clapped at their teasing of me.

On a hot Saturday morning as I sat on my verandah, several of the staff's children who lived nearby spied me and clambered on the porch. While we laughed and talked, the little girls plaited each other's hair, creating twisted black spikes on their tiny heads.

By *talked,* I don't mean with words. It amazed me that we could communicate even though I hadn't begun my study of the language yet and knew only a limited number of Chichewa words and phrases. We gestured a lot. So I pointed to my head to inquire if they wanted to plait my hair. Their eyes lit up with delight. A burst of little hands grabbed for my head—but they jumped back, screaming: "EEE!" and "WAH!" at the strange feel of my soft hair strands. As they attempted to plait it, my hair kept flopping over and wouldn't stand upright as theirs did. They studied me, arms akimbo, their frowning faces confirming a serious flaw in me they just discovered.

I wondered if I was the first white woman they had been invited to touch.

It was not only with children that I learned other nonverbal ways to communicate with people of another language. Often in the months ahead I felt I was understanding what a Malawian was saying, though I didn't know all the words they were using. Something at a deeper level was happening—a pre-verbal connection with them that I relished.

In later times in Tengani village, where I lived for three months, I would spend hours visiting with Asena women, who spoke a different dialect than the one I knew. We gestured and laughed a lot at my stumbling attempts to mimic their words.

*

Several weeks into my time in Phalombe, I summarized my first impressions for a friend in the States:

Dear Katherine,

...I'm really taken aback by the poverty and primitiveness of it all, the everywhere presence of preventable diseases, the physical and psychic isolation of our community, days full of sweat and insects, the inherent frustrations of medical work here. The medicine men send us their failed patients about to die. Hygiene, as we know it, is unknown.

How will I ever adapt and learn what is real here, what things mean underneath their appearance?

Yet there is so much beauty woven through these defying circumstances: the magnificent African night sky bursting with southern stars, the bleaching sun, the touching politeness and friendliness of the Malawian people. They always greet each other and me when *passing on the road; they smile and laugh in spite of the physical burdens of this environment and the deep fears and taboos that taint daily events.*

I have been sick several times since being here: viral colds, headaches, persistent diarrhea, and stomach upset. It all seems to be part of the adjustment process. I just hope I don't get malaria. If I can survive these primal confrontations, I believe I will grow to love this country and its people.

Well, Katherine, some of my little neighbor girls are outside on the porch calling for me, so I must end. They come to the house once a week for sewing lessons that I started for them. Funny to think of me, of all people, teaching sewing—and it's hard for them with a left-handed teacher.

*

Entry into Malawian culture was proving to be less difficult than into the community culture in Phalombe. The majority of the Dutch sisters were middle-aged and had lived through the occupation of their country during World War II. Tough, heavy-footed women, they didn't tolerate anything that smacked of softness. I think they considered Americans a spoiled people.

Those sisters became nuns before the Catholic Church's Vatican II days of change in the late sixties, while my spirituality was a product of that decade. Between them and the four of us in the Pilot Project a gap yawned, not only of world views, but of religious perspectives.

I was not prepared for my own community of sisters to be my biggest challenge.

By 1969 we no longer wore religious habits—just Western dresses, skirts,

and blouses, or white uniforms. Whenever I could, I wore the local *nsaru*, a richly patterned cotton cloth, as a long skirt to cover my legs, topped with a simple blouse. In Malawian culture, it was immodest for a woman to show much of her legs, although they often went topless. Breasts were practical body parts used for nursing and didn't carry sexual connotations. Wearing the *nsaru* was my way to honor the culture and connect to the people, and my gesture seemed to be appreciated by the Malawians. The sisters, however, criticized me for "dressing native."

It seemed that each day brought another opportunity for someone to fault me: I salted my food before I tasted it (the food was so bland); I used tissues during my many colds rather than the more economical (but unhygienic) hanky; I spent too much time visiting with the student nurses . . . on and on. One day I put a note on the main house bulletin board inviting the sisters to join the students in an evening of singing. The note disappeared without explanation.

I was not discouraged by the tremendous heat or the crawling, flying creatures, or the lack of electricity, but the slow drip of criticism steadily wore down my spirit. I used my journals to file my complaints:

> I don't like that the sisters call our male staff "boys."
> They don't seem to know much about the culture and
> many of them don't speak Chichewa fluently, even
> after being here for years. They seem to want to create
> a little Holland here. I don't want either Holland or
> America—I want to be in Malawi. This is the whole
> point of our Pilot Project—to connect with the people,
> become a part of their world.

There was an unspoken belief in the missionary community that the Malawian culture was less evolved; to adapt to it was to regress. I believed that true evolution had to do with the human spirit, not material mastery. I didn't believe the West was evolving in a straight, upward trajectory; not everything we called progress was advancement. Material culture was not the same as human values, and I found so many positive qualities in the Malawian people that were declining in the West. I feared even more that we outside do-gooders were somehow altering the culture of those people in ways that could ultimately be more destructive than positive—like eroding their confidence in themselves, their values, and making them feel dependent on outsiders. How could one support needed development without introducing foreign values that intrude and corrupt?

My discomfort with my community of sisters and the conflicts embedded in differing world views deepened as the weeks and months passed. As the only American in the early days before a second sister arrived from the States, I felt the brunt of the Dutch sisters' discomfort with the Pilot Project, which was developed in 1968 by a team of American Medical Mission Sisters with academic consultants. The formal name of the Pilot Project was the Cultural Orientation Program Experiment (COPE) and, as with all experiments, much was unknown, untried, and risky. The intent was to apply the growing knowledge about the role of culture to the orientation of sisters newly arrived at their host missions. Young members from several countries were selected to participate in a nine-month orientation program—me being one of them—to test out an experience-based approach to language learning and cultural adaptation.

What I didn't know then was that there were warning signs about placing the COPE Pilot Project in Malawi. There had been serious miscommunications between the US planners and the Dutch sisters, who had many fears and concerns about the project and perceived it as prematurely imposed on them. The arrival of MMS from other cultures threatened their own cultural identity. Work, their primary value, was challenged by the prolonged academic and cultural immersion structured into the Pilot Project. According to them, the newly arrived sisters weren't productive and didn't contribute sufficiently to the medical work. We were also too independent, unwilling to conform to the mores of the larger, conservative Dutch Catholic missionary community. It was a classic clash of world views and proved extremely painful and difficult for everyone involved. The effort to integrate three different home cultures in daily living—Dutch, American, and Filipino—was a challenge in itself, but there was also the additional layer of the larger missionary culture, and of primary importance, the Malawian culture.

The older, more traditional sisters made major contributions to medical care and training in Malawi over many years, but still caught in a colonialist mentality, they lived in a Dutch enclave and did not readily enter the lives of the Malawian people outside of their work. I believed that empowering people to manage their own environment by showing mutual respect and working side by side as equals was the best way to positively contribute to a developing country.

One could argue over which was the better approach.

Sister Miriam did what she could to support the Pilot Project participants, but she was often caught between the Dutch sisters' expectations and the needs of us newcomers. And needs I surely had in those days of such profound adjustments. My journal was often the companion I turned to when sorting through my experiences. The following is one of my many discouraged journal entries:

> It's raining today—first time in over a month.
> Everyone hopes it will last long enough to save
> the local bean crop. I have been really down today,
> crying so much that I skipped our afternoon language
> class and holed up in my bedroom. Living in this
> community is so difficult because there is always some
> major misunderstanding about the simplest things.
> Yet nothing is discussed; I just hear about an issue
> secondhand. I spend so much energy trying to be
> diplomatic. Feeling so unsupported sours everything for
> me. I feel my aloneness down to my toes.

I gave up so much in the hopes of finding more here in Africa. It saddens me that the very thing I expect and need my community to be, it's not. The sisters seem oblivious of the religious renewal that is taking place throughout the Western world. The superior is still the sole decision-maker and we are expected to ask permission for everything, even toiletries. I spoke with her and told her I just couldn't relate in the dependent way the others do.

I'm so tired of all this small-mindedness and feel so many defenses rising in me in reaction to it all. I hate to see this in myself. I never expected to feel so ill at ease with my own sisters.

I wonder what it means that I feel more at home with the Malawians than with my own religious community?

CHAPTER TWENTY-NINE

NEW FRIENDS

Several challenging weeks after my arrival, while the sun hung low in the sky, Miriam and the four of us newcomers climbed into the rickety ambulance for the two-mile drive to Likulezi Catechetical Training Center, established for the preparation of Malawian lay ministers. In just a few more days we would begin daily commutes there for our three-month language and culture course taught by its director, Father Prinsen, a world-renowned anthropologist and Dutch priest.

Excited and nervous about meeting Father Prinsen, I hadn't anticipated the beauty of his surroundings; the foothills of the majestic Mulanje Mountains seemed to rise straight up from his verandah. The gardens and shade trees surrounding the house created an idyllic setting. It was such a contrast to our own rustic compound a short distance away. I wished I could live there instead.

Father was a pouchy, graying man with a pleasant face framed by cauliflower ears. For someone so renowned, he displayed an unassuming demeanor, though his eyebrows lifted slightly as a silent reaction to what others said. At the start of that introductory visit he appeared a bit uncomfortable with us. It was the first time he would be teaching young, non-Dutch sisters in that new collaborative venture with Medical Mission Sisters in the US and Phalombe.

I had expected to be intimidated and lost for words around him—he *was* the foremost scholar of Malawian culture—but I wasn't. I felt a surprising ease as I peppered him with questions, which he seemed to appreciate.

After seeing the site for our classes and meeting Father, I was chomping at the bit to start our studies about the Malawian people, who were to become *my people*. I had been looking in from the outside over the past weeks, and I wanted to be inside their world.

Toward the end of our visit, Father briefly mentioned that six newly arrived Dutch priests would be joining us in the course. I wondered what they would be like, how old, and if I would feel comfortable with them.

Before we left that day, Father Prinsen invited us to watch the wives of his students perform a local dance. A group of about twenty-five Malawian men and women were gathered in a tree-shaded courtyard on the property. While the men drummed, the women, several with babies tied on their backs, swayed and stomped in a circle to the pounding rhythm.

One woman left the ring of pulsing bodies when her baby started crying. I gestured to her if I could hold her little one so she could continue to dance. The fussy infant was adorable, though quite messy—a runny nose and a coating of dust and clay on his dark skin. He quieted in my arms, perhaps shocked into silence by the white face smiling down at him. The mother rejoined the dancers, lighter in her movement; I sat, happier holding a child.

Finally, on March 2—the day couldn't come too soon—our first class convened on the verandah of Father's house. With the start of the course, my Likulezi classmates became a third circle of relationships, along with my sister community and the Malawians.

Pat, another American, arrived in Phalombe just at the start of the classes. She bridged my singleness. We were now five sisters in the Pilot Project studying with the six Dutch priests, several recently ordained. In our twenties and thirties, my classmates and I epitomized the new breed of religious missionaries, and we quickly discovered an easy commonality in spite of coming from three different countries. With many opportunities to be together, whether tentatively practicing Chichewa, sharing prayer services we created, or talking about the work we hoped to do, our friendships widened and deepened. What I hadn't found among the Phalombe sisters, I found in that peer group.

All the young Dutch priests were friendly and talkative, but I was especially drawn to Gerard, who at thirty-three was the oldest of the group and had been an ordained priest for eight years. With his dark glasses framing his deep brown eyes, he looked like the scholar he was, as well as like a monk with his tonsured head and fringe of sandy blond hair. I felt immediately comfortable with him and appreciated his maturity, humor, and kindness, as well as the depth of discussions we came to share. I also secretly admired how professorial he looked with his pipe perched on his lips or cradled in his hand when he spoke in class.

We newcomers were so zealous, ready to delve into our cultural studies and to begin using Chichewa to interact more fully with the locals. We shared a Vatican II theory of mission work that focused on respect for indigenous cultures and the recognition that we came not just to give, but also to receive and learn from the Malawians. For us, respectful relationships and loving service, not domination, were the motivation behind our presence. The fiery evangelist with a raised cross in a clenched fist was not our vision of the missionary calling.

Our classes and conversations generated many reflections in my journal:

> I am frightened by the prospect of becoming a colonialist like some of the missionaries I see around me. At times they speak critically of the Malawians, belittling them. It pains me.

*

> How do I separate my religious from my cultural values? How do I share the essential Christian message without mixing it with the incidentals of Western institutional religion?

*

*How do I experience the raw asceticism of living
in another culture and strip down to my spiritual
core? What does my vow of poverty mean here in
Malawi, where there is such a lack of material
necessities, conveniences, and comfort in the lives of
the people compared to what I have?*

These questions were on all of our minds and surfaced in our serious conversations during class breaks and in our shared prayer services. We studied hard, driven by the desire to become the presence we wanted to be in the culture, but we also enjoyed each other's company, the delight of discovering new friends.

One Saturday in the middle of March when we had no class, the group of us decided to hike one side of the Mulanje Mountains.

The climb required that I use my body as never before; my arms stretched for rocks and branches above me, my toes dug for a hold on the slopes, my eyes scanned for the easiest footing. The sense of distance and relationship to the terrain kept shifting during the several hours we climbed. I was exhilarated to reach the top, where we found a dilapidated hut in which to rest and eat the lunch we had packed. There on the mountain ridge we laughed out of sheer pleasure at having succeeded in getting there.

When it was time to begin our descent a light rain began to fall, making the rocky side of the stream we had to shimmy down extremely slippery. Staring down the sloped route we had to take and seeing the land drop away, my fear of heights kicked in and panic rooted me to the spot. Noting the terror in my eyes, Gerard told the others to go ahead of us. He stayed with me during the ten minutes it took to reach a more level spot, his one arm wrapped around my waist, coaxing me as we inched our way down in a sitting position.

That experience marked the first time since I had been in Malawi that I felt cared for.

I wrote about the climb the next day:

*The thrill of making it up and down the mountain
filled me with an unfamiliar joy at the sheer*

physicality of the day. I rarely use my body, push its limits, really don't even think about it, until yesterday on the climb.

Last evening as I scanned my skin for sore places, I was surprised by my firm muscles and soft curves. It was the first time that I have examined my naked body.

It's an occupational hazard of celibacy that I don't consider my body a part of my self, don't use it for anything other than work. Yet the climb was an outlet to express my physical being, as was the dancing I did with the student nurses. While my body will not find expression in a sexual way because of my vow of celibacy, I need to find more ways to acknowledge it as part of ME.

I didn't record anything in my journal about how Gerard's concern and support on the mountaintop affected me. That was a silent stream running beneath my consciousness.

*

The three months of culture and language studies passed much too quickly. I still felt like a baby colt on shaky linguistic legs when the course ended, and I had just begun to crack into the Malawian culture. While my bilingual classmates achieved good basic language skills, I felt like I was in the "dada, mama" stage of Chichewa.

In early June we had a simple graduation ceremony with the superiors of our two religious communities looking on. They joined in our class photo with Father Prinsen, our two Chichewa mentors, Edward and Mary, and our classmates. It was difficult to say good-bye. We had all grown so close over the past months.

The six priests were to leave Likulezi the day after graduation for their various mission assignments further south in the Lower Shire, while the five of us in the MMS Pilot Project were to begin two weeks of solo language immersion in different communities of Malawian nuns.

On the day the course ended, Gerard handed me a letter to read later:

Dear Aimee,

I think you will be surprised when you receive this letter. I reflected a long time if I should do so, but at last I got convinced that it will be good. The aim of this: last Friday we had deep talks about what it means to be a Christian, what will be expected from each of us to follow the appeal of the gospel, what does fidelity to our vocation mean, and where is the line between freedom and responsibility. All these questions are for me—and I think, for you—a living reality.

Perhaps you remember my remark on Friday evening that I hate to be alone; on the other hand, I really like my work as a priest.

You may be surprised that I am so confidential to you; the reason is that I like you, because you are in my eyes a real woman who can understand things like this and it will be clear to you that, especially in the loneliness of a tropical country, one needs somebody to share with. The other priests speak only of work.

If you don't mind, I will like to write you occasionally. I think it is worthful to have a real friend to trust with the secrets of the heart, but please tell me if you don't like it; be honest; take your freedom. Never in my life I'll blame you for it.

I hope we will find a certain measure of faith in the future. I wish you all the best and good luck with your Chichewa practice in Muloza.

Yours, Gerard (Sorry for my bad English.)

I was touched that Gerard, though six years older, perceived me as a confidant. I responded with a letter to him at Nsanje mission, where he had just arrived, assuring him of my willingness to be the listening ear he needed. I told him I valued the depth of our friendship as well, and my experience in the course had been enriched by our talks. I sent him a photo—so he could remember me—as I had no sense that we would meet again. Nsanje was a distant outpost in the far south of the country about six or seven hours from Phalombe, with the dangerous Cholo escarpment in-between. I was heading for two weeks to Muloza mission on the border of Portuguese East Africa. Our near futures—let alone the distant ones—were unknowable.

A second letter awaited me in Phalombe when I returned from my two weeks' stay in Muloza:

Dear Aimee,

I cannot describe what happened in me at the moment of seeing your foto and reading your letter. I read it four times. Indeed, our friendship was unexpected, unhoped for, precious. The past three months at Likulezi were for me a happy time, and you were especially the one who was the source of my happiness because of your spontaneity, your cordiality, your feelings as a woman. You take pleasure in the people you meet, the little things you do and see.

I don't know how you feel, but I must say, I miss you, your kindness, our discussions. I am thankful that I could meet you.

Aimee, all the best. God be with you,
Gerard

When I felt I was riding a wobbly raft in the turbulent seas of Phalombe, Gerard's subsequent letters became an anchor, a reminder that I had a good friend in the south of the country.

CHAPTER THIRTY

AFRICA GETS INSIDE ME

After Father Prinsen's course I decided to spend the next phase of our Pilot Project—language immersion—at the Muloza mission, a two-hour drive on the other side of the Mulanje Mountains. Our Phalombe hospital supervised a maternity clinic managed by African sisters there. I planned to live with them for two weeks, practice my Chichewa, and learn about their lives.

Muloza was a small Catholic outpost bordering what we called "Portuguese," an abbreviated name for Portuguese East Africa, which would become Mozambique in 1975. The Dutch priest in charge at Muloza was Father De Groot, a short, stocky man with warm eyes and a graying beard. I described him as an old man in a letter home, but I later learned he was only forty-five. I didn't know his first name; he was always Father De Groot to me.

The African sisters in Malawi had adopted traditional forms of Western religious life, wearing long heavy habits despite the tropical climate. I thought it unfortunate that their religious lifestyle wasn't adapted to their own environment and traditions.

Muloza mission.

I originally intended to live with the sisters, but Father suggested that their living conditions would be too difficult for me. They slept on floor mats, and their diet and food preparation could be problematic for my unaccustomed stomach. He felt it wisest that I spend my days with the sisters but sleep and eat at the guest quarters in his house.

Neither Father nor I could have anticipated that our relationship would evolve into one of tender companionship that, at the time, I was too naive to fully appreciate. Our closeness, arising from an unexpected circumstance, created a childlike reliance on him. He was a tender father, but also a man to the woman he saw, a quality still hidden from me.

June 1970 journal:

> After my first few days in Muloza Sister Maria, the superior, told me that all the sisters had talked and they didn't feel they were helping me with my Chichewa. I think the truth is that it's me who has failed to make the effort. I am so uncomfortable; I feel like a mentally impaired child among them and have to push myself to be with them. I understand so little of their Chichewa conversation, and only two speak any English. The silence among us creates a void that feels embarrassing. I can get just so far with hand signs and baby words. I've hidden myself in my language book rather than mix with them. What am I doing here?

Early in my stay I accompanied Father and one of the sisters to the outlying Pheremwe village church. Shortly into the rugged hour's ride, my stomach became quite upset, aggravated by the washboard roads. My companions, noticing my discomfort, insinuated that I was a softie. As we walked around the village, I fell into a brooding silence; I felt passive and discouraged, unable to rouse myself to speak more Chichewa with the local people and berating myself for it.

Later at Mass, Father entreated the congregation to contribute more generously toward the church he was building. I was reminded of typical Catholic parishes at home where the priests seemed to focus on money. I didn't believe that the church was a building, but a community of people. They could meet outside under a tree.

> I feel a discrepancy between the "Good News" of the gospels and that artificial overlay of Christianity

on the Malawians. It's become a widening gap in my mind.

Perhaps I should return home to the States; I'm miserable and incompetent. Am I too idealistic, too unrealistic about my abilities to cope with the demands here in Malawi? Maybe Father is right and I am too soft for this missionary life. I'm really worried now about the coming plan to live in a village for three months when I leave here.

The next day I fell into the clutches of malaria in spite of the preventive chloroquine tablets I faithfully swallowed. It was the first of three bouts, and the most serious one. Its onset helped to explain my discomfort the day before.

The symptoms held me captive in bed for days; alternating chills and fever that shook my body, left me drained of energy to even move, and gave me a headache that smashed my eyes closed. During those racking days and nights, Father tenderly nursed me, bringing medicines, cold cloths for my hot forehead, and blankets for my chills. In the beginning I couldn't hold down any food, but after a few days, I was able to swallow spoonfuls of the light soups he brought.

I felt so guilty for burdening him when I had come to live with the sisters.

Though still weak, I began to join Father at his table for meals when I could get up and walk. Over the following four days of my gradual recovery we talked of many things: our pasts, our families in the States and the Netherlands, the Church in Malawi and the challenges of living there. Years later I remember, not the details of our conversations, but the tender warmth of our times together, the easy sharing.

Finally able to get out of bed for longer periods, I would spend cool evenings with Father in front of his living room fireplace. We sat across from each other; he reading, while I was too weak to do more than stare into the flames. At times his book or my thoughts would spark a comment or reflection.

Living there in such a primal environment, pangs of the most basic human instincts surfaced in me—like my fascination with fire: getting lost in the flames, staring for an hour into their depth, intuiting ancestral ties, something ancient in the furtive flicks of orange and blue arms that reached for me.

I can still remember that fire, being seduced by it, especially there in Africa where open fires lit the night for cooking, or warmth, or dancing and drumming circles. Those mystical nights by the fireplace with Father De Groot nurtured my recovery. Much later I discovered how deeply meaningful they were for him, as well.

Over those days of improvement I often jotted notes in my journal to capture my fleeting thoughts and pass the time in bed:

> I'm grappling to find some basic trust in myself. Before
> I came to Malawi, all I desired was to live in Africa,
> offer my nursing skills, and create connection between
> yet unknown people and myself. Now I'm finally
> here among them, but I'm filled with conflicting
> reactions. As I hear Father belittle the people out of his
> frustrations yet devote his life to them, I wonder if his
> concrete efforts are better than my theoretical concepts?
> I think that our love for these Malawians must be
> enfleshed in relationships, not concrete blocks... but
> what do I know? My thoughts are so untested.

Once I recovered I spent time visiting with the sisters and seemed to understand more of their conversation. It was a minor breakthrough, due perhaps to the rise of energy and optimism. I had let go of my sense of failure and preoccupation with how the others judged me. I was sick those days, not only with malaria, but also with some persistent stomach bug that left me continuously nauseated. Coupled with my struggles to speak Chichewa, my stay had been a bruising experience for my ego and confidence.

I knew that I had to see all that as temporary rather than questioning my life's calling as I had been doing.

I also marveled at the extraordinary situation I was in and the experiences it afforded me. I'll always remember one day shortly before I left, sitting on a large rock on the mountainside looking out over the Muloza plain with one of the younger sisters. There I was with my new friend, perched on the border of Malawi and Portuguese East Africa. Me—Rie from Philadelphia.

June 27, 1970, was my parents' wedding anniversary and my next to the last night in Muloza. Father offered the Mass for them and even mentioned their anniversary in his homily during the service. That night, he prepared a seemingly romantic evening: a delicious spaghetti dinner complete with Portuguese wine, flowers from his garden, and music on his record player.

In my journal that night I wrote, "I felt like it was *my* anniversary."

I left Muloza two days later, knowing I had failed to achieve the goal of that phase of the Pilot Project—significant improvement in speaking and understanding Chichewa—but I was changed by my time there, in ways I could neither understand nor explain.

CHAPTER THIRTY-ONE

BONFIRE IN THE NIGHT

When I returned from Muloza to Phalombe I only had a few days to prepare to move to Tengani, in the far south of the country, for the next phase of the Pilot Project. For three months I would live with Norma and Yoli in the heart of a village researching the culture and improving our Chichewa. I didn't know if I would succeed in such a venture; it had never been done before in our community of sisters. Fathers Gerard and Pieter from our Likulezi course were stationed about an hour south of Tengani and said they would help us as they were able. It had been Gerard's suggestion to ask his bishop if we could use Father Van Horne's empty house for that village immersion phase of our project.

*

At sunrise on July 2 Norma, Yoli, and I, with Sinas driving, pulled away from the familiar Phalombe compound. When I climbed into that vehicle, a life-changing personal journey was set in motion.

The loaded ambulance, bulging with four people and boxes of supplies and luggage, plodded along the rutted roads like an arthritic fat lady. With the familiar Mulanje Mountains as backdrop, we bumped and bounced like sacks of potatoes across vast stretches of tree-studded grasslands and through the center of sleepy Blantyre.

The daunting Cholo escarpment awaited us: a narrow, twisting mountain road littered with boulders. Its snaking course taunted us with abrupt precipices, prompting us to instinctively shift our weight away from the sheer drops. Farther into the tortuous route and nearing our final descent we caught fleeting glimpses of the shimmering Shire Plain in the distance, the hottest and most desolate region in Malawi. But for us on the treacherous massif, it promised safety. Only when we slid onto the flat landscape at the bottom could we relax. We had survived.

After less than an hour of driving we made a sharp right turn into the Muona compound, home of the bishop and a Catholic hospital run by European sisters, to pay a courtesy call. Over coffee and bananas we chatted with the bishop. We thanked him for letting us use the vacated village house of Father Van Horne, one of his priests, for that third stage of the Pilot Project—digging deeper into the daily life of the ordinary Malawian.

As we readied to get back on the road to Tengani, the bishop shook his head in a gesture suggesting both admiration and concern for the three of us living alone in a village. Most Catholic sisters lived together in larger communities. But the bishop wished us well and gifted us with a dozen freshly laid eggs and flowers from his garden.

Back on the road the scenery soon changed into the barren, cattle-dotted countryside of the Lower Shire (pronounced Sheer-ee), named after the river that slithered through the land on its way to the Zambezi River and the Indian Ocean. A setting sun turned the water into gold beads as the ferry man pulled us across the river in jerking movements, our creaky old ambulance rocking on the boat's narrow wooden platform. Standing at its prow I felt like an early explorer venturing into an untamed new world.

Delivered onto dry land, we met small herds of bony cattle and bleating goats ambling along the sandy road. As dusk descended we feared we were lost—the drive felt much longer than expected—but two boys on the road assured our driver that Tengani was nearby. "Look for two abandoned Indian stores," they said.

We were not surprised that they were abandoned. Once elected in 1964, President Kamuzu Banda had been promoting the ouster of Asian merchants in favor of native Malawians. He had also recently banished the Peace Corps from the country.

Sinas peered through the front window of our vehicle as we turned into the village on a narrower dirt road and inched through a maze of shadowed huts searching for Father Van Horne's empty cinderblock house. Midway through a large clearing we passed a boisterous crowd dancing to throbbing drumbeats, their bodies glistened by the flashing orange flames of a leaping bonfire.

The primeval night scene frightened me. *What had I gotten myself into?*

When we reached the house, the band of boys who had been running alongside us circled and stared at the strange white women alighting from the back of the ambulance. They clamored to tell us that two *bambos* (fathers) had been waiting to greet us, but left a short while before. In that moment I would have given anything to have been welcomed by their familiar faces.

Johan, the cook and caretaker of the house, was expecting us and arrived to unlock the door while the young boys jostled to transfer our things into the house. Once inside the little box that was to be our home we sent Johan and the boys away with tired words of thanks, plopped in the middle of the suitcases and bags strewn over the floor, and devoured the dry cheese sandwiches we had brought. I was exhausted and overwhelmed, close to crying, but also able to tap into a deeper courage within me.

Our two priest friends from Nsanje had been there and left us a near-empty thermos of coffee, flowers, grapefruits, a book called *How to Survive,* and a logbook where they wrote the following message on the first page. We would faithfully record every day of our three months in Tengani village in that book:

2 July 1970

Feast of the Visitation of Mary to her cousin Elizabeth

According to Mary's example in the scriptures, we came with haste over the plain to help our relative ... well .. our dear friends.

We arrived at Tengani village early afternoon bearing a cake from the sisters in Nsanje, and we readied coffee for what we expected would be your imminent arrival. However, after waiting and waiting, after playing football with the children and watching their dances, who still did not appear on the stage? You, the sisters from Phalombe.

Dusk is upon us. After drinking most of your coffee and eating the cake, we decided to go home. We know the trip down the Cholo escarpment can be dangerous, so we hope you are safe.

Gerard plans to see you here on Sunday morning and will bring you to Nsanje to do any necessary shopping.

Wishing the three of you a fruitful, blessed stay in the house of dear Father Van Horne, our brother priest,

Pieter and Gerard

I was especially relieved that Gerard would be coming to help us. I had developed a confidence in him over the months we were together in Likulezi for our studies. He had an appealing way with both adults and children and had developed a facility with Chichewa far better than mine.

While hungrily eating we surveyed our simple abode, built by an earlier missionary: plastered walls grayed by time and a rough concrete floor. Candles and kerosene lanterns lit up our evenings, as we had no electricity. Poorly sealed glass windows let in heat and sand, as we would later discover with the sandstorms that enveloped the village. A small screened porch protected us from most of the flying insects, but I saw far too many hairy spiders dangling on their webs in every room.

Heartened by the gifts that greeted us and our hunger assuaged, we summoned enough energy to shift some of our things into the appropriate rooms, then chose our beds and found toothbrushes, matches, and lanterns. There was no water coming from the spigots, so we couldn't wash off the trip's dust. We shared our last bottle of water to brush our teeth.

I sketched the layout of the tiny house in our logbook (*konde* is Chichewa for porch).

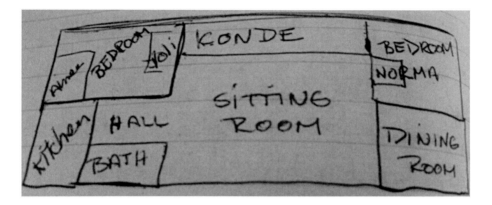

Once my mosquito net was hung, I collapsed into bed bone-weary yet unable to sleep, disquieted by the drums and voices haunting the dark beyond our little box.

Malawi was so far from everywhere—and Tengani was far away from everywhere else in Malawi.

Scenes from Tengani Village.

CHAPTER THIRTY-TWO

THE FISHBOWL

The caretaker's knock woke us early. Accustomed to working for Father Van Horne, Johan walked in uninvited and insisted on helping, although he only added to our first morning's confusion. While we tried to cobble together a breakfast we placated him with the task of boiling coffee.

That first day we began what was to become our daily ritual of praying together at breakfast, asking for the grace to be receptive to everyone and fearless to what that day would bring. How unsuspecting we were of the constant demands that openness would invite.

Gerard was our first guest that next day, come to welcome us and see what we might need. A letter sent home in July 1970 revealed a subconscious shift in my relationship with him that I hadn't yet noticed:

> On the second day after we arrived here in Tengani,
> Gerard showed up to see how we were getting on, and
> I could have kissed him. It was such a relief to have a
> man around. He fixed our refrigerator, gave us some
> advice from what he had learned so far about living
> in the Lower Shire, and listened to our stories and
> concerns.

Along with Gerard's many visits, our house soon became the center of attention in the village, a stopping point for all the missionaries and expatriates traveling between Blantyre and Nsanje. Well into our three-month stay, two Malawians dropped by with a foreign visitor whom they said they were taking to "all the places of interest in the Lower Shire."

How surprised we were to discover that we and our little house had become a tourist stop.

As for Johan, a well-intentioned but self-important man, he continued to intrude into our days—usually at very early hours—for our entire stay. Though we wanted to be self-reliant, we soon learned we needed his knowledge and skills, so we endured his argumentative and meddlesome behavior. I came to appreciate him and his persistence when the heat alone was enough to collapse a person into an unmovable lump.

Sinas, who had slept elsewhere that night, came that first morning to assemble our one bike, then with the sun rising to mid-sky, he readied to return to Phalombe. When he shifted in the front seat of the ambulance to wave good-bye, I wanted to climb in with him and forsake our mad venture.

What were we doing, three single women living in a village, the only white faces for miles, an hour from the nearest town—with only one bike? What would we do in an emergency?

Yet we stayed—abandoned by choice.

We quickly threw ourselves into cleaning away the veneer of dust and sand and settling in. My frustration level ramped up when we couldn't find basic things we needed and didn't know how to work the two-burner cooktop or small refrigerator, both run on kerosene. Though simple in design, the aged pieces would frequently break down during our stay, and we often ran out of kerosene or wicks. That first morning, the fridge was not working, so we feared that the precious supply of meat we had brought would spoil . . . which it did.

Boiling our water and cooking on two burners required more time than we anticipated, and our limited food stock and poor cooking skills resulted in barely edible meals. We quickly learned that just to get water in the spigots was a time-intensive process.

Johan paid a few village girls to bring buckets of water—on their heads—from the bore hole a mile away. He refused to do "women's work." His job was to empty the delivered buckets into a large tank outside the house and then pump the water up to another tank on the roof. Voilà—cold water flowed from the spigots and shower head. Over the coming months we were frequently without water: problems with truculent Johan, or the often broken pump. We then had to haul buckets of water inside while waiting days for a replacement part. The toilet also overflowed numerous times, spilling the precious liquid over the floor and reaching as far as the other side of the house. Many nights I fell into bed without a shower and only a bucket of water to rinse the village dust and sweat from my sticky skin. The impact of limited access to clean water for us—as for most Africans—was one of many daily hardships.

The reality of village life soon seeped into my body, making every quotidian task a major consumer of time and energy. In those early days, I was exhausted and frazzled trying to cope with the unending inconveniences, and I felt helpless when my rudimentary Chichewa failed me. That language issue was compounded by the discovery that our neighbors belonged to the Asena tribe and spoke Chisena. No wonder I couldn't understand them. Fortunately, they also spoke the national language of Chichewa and soon learned to use that dialect with us.

In the midst of our disorientation that first day, a multitude of wide-eyed children, fascinated by the strange *azungu* (white foreigners), peered through the windows and doors to watch us. A single male missionary was all they had seen. The flock of chattering children encircled our house *every* day for three months, making us the proverbial fish in a glass bowl. That lack of privacy drained my reservoir more than anything else. It proved challenging to find time alone until sometime very late at night when all I could manage was to crash into bed.

In a place where nothing new happened, we were a novelty. Every move we made was known throughout the village and beyond—we had no escape from prying eyes and eager ears. Our goings and comings were the spoken headlines of each day.

Besides the ever-present children and teens, a steady stream of adults, perceiving us as a resource for every need, came to our door: an ancient man begging for money, someone needing a stamp, a boy with a bucket of goat's milk, another with eggs to sell or chickens or corn—whatever might bring them a few coins.

We had a small budget for our stay in Tengani and always bought from the locals when we could, giving as generously as we could. As the treasurer of our little venture, I kept track of our expenditures in the back of the logbook, most of it paid out in the local equivalent of US pennies and nickels.

Our new neighbors also had so many medical needs: a boy who knocked late one morning with a fish hook in his lip that Norma delicately removed; a limping woman with an oozing leg ulcer that I cleaned and bandaged. The unending requests for medicine for rampant skin infections, diarrhea, wounds, and unknown pains wore me down. The villagers' needs engulfed me. Though all three of us were medically trained—Yoli a pharmacist, Norma a doctor, I a nurse, we weren't there to practice our professions in that phase of the Pilot Project, but rather to study values and behaviors to accommodate our future medical care to those we wanted to serve. But it pained me to see how much these long-suffering people endured. How unfair that they died from conditions that were easily treated back home.

Most days I felt empty-handed in the face of their unrelenting needs. In spite of the many small things I did to help them—it was never enough.

But not all the requests that came to our door were problems. Some were celebrations of life.

Shortly after sunrise one morning, we heard a knock. The man's cow was having a difficult labor and he wanted us to help her deliver. I shot Norma, our doctor, a quizzical look. She demurred on the unfamiliar obstetrical situation but suggested by gestures that he might try pulling the breach calf out by its protruding legs. Encouraged, he jumped on his bike to try that.

He returned the next day to report he successfully delivered a female calf. We were aunts!

A few days later, another man rapped on our window to inform us that his goat was in labor on the roadway. Curious city girls, we raced out, Norma's camera swinging from her neck. Because we showed up, a crowd soon gathered. Norma snapped away to their utter amazement—what was so noteworthy about a goat being born? She and I *oohed* and *aahed* as, not one, but two kids came slithering out. They were up on their wobbly legs almost immediately, their umbilical cords hanging from their bellies, the placenta still in the mother. As the newborn kids stumbled and bumped into each other, the tugs on the cords helped release the placenta, which then laid on the dirt and was slowly consumed by the she-goat.

The various animals owned by the local people, like those goats, were our main source of protein: a chicken that skittered by me as I walked through the village might end up on our dinner table a few days later. Initially they were brought to us flapping and squawking, hanging upside down from the hand of the seller, but our neighbors soon learned that we were too squeamish and needed to have chickens DOA—decapitated on arrival.

One of the locals brought us his cow's milk for several weeks, but in mid-August the cow's owner came to apologize that he couldn't bring any that day. The source of the milk had taken an unannounced stroll into the bush and couldn't be found.

Eggs and goat meat were also available, as were corn meal, rice and sweet potatoes, bananas and papaya. Most of our vegetables came from a can or as gifts from the missionaries who had gardens. Our eating habits and quantity of food surpassed what the local people had. The Malawians only ate two meals a day, in the afternoon and evening, working all morning on empty stomachs.

On many of my walks through the neighborhood under the broiling 110-degree sun I might be handed a papaya or two eggs. Those people who had so little were still so generous. I was quite happy, however, that a woman skinning a monkey didn't offer me a piece of it as I passed.

In our first few weeks before a car was loaned us, our food came from our Tengani neighbors and the one local Malawian-owned store that carried a few dry goods like salt, sugar, and flour, along with diverse items like bicycle tires, cloths, and machetes. Our diet was greatly improved by traveling missionaries who, sympathetic to our isolation, brought us food. When he had time, Gerard drove us to Nsanje for groceries before we had a car. Over our months there he was thoughtful and generous, often bringing us mail, food, flowers, and news of what was going on in other parts of the Lower Shire.

We drank Fanta, a bottled orange drink sold locally, milk from our neighbor's cow, and wine and beer bought over the border in "Portuguese." I also sampled the local brew, *mowa* (beer), and even sipped the occasionally offered home-distilled *kachasu*, a hard liquor.

Witnessing my neighbors' daily activities on my strolls, I sought ways to experience their realities. How did the women manage to carry their babies on their backs? A mother let me practice with her infant and her *nsaru*—a seemingly simple act that proved extremely challenging. I had to bend over and balance the little one on my back while using both hands to quickly pull up the cloth from behind, so the baby wouldn't slide off before I secured it, then anchored the bottom of the fabric so it wouldn't come undone and cause the infant to drop to the ground. What marvels those women were, walking long distances, pounding grains, and hoeing, all with the added weight of a baby attached to their backs.

On another walk I came across women pounding maize in large wooden mortars hollowed out of tree trunks. They would gather in a circle and chant, the rhythm helping them control their breathing and pace the lifting of the heavy wooden pestles up and down to grind the maize. I tried to do it and could hardly pick up the deadweight pole.

As several of the women were lifting the baskets of pounded grain onto their heads, I asked if I could try that. They laughed knowingly—I was in for a surprise. First they laid a woven grass donut on my head, and then two women lifted a basket up to it. My neck buckled and they quickly had to lift it off. I have a deformed cervical vertebrae to this day that testifies to the basket's leaden weight.

Though they looked so scrawny and thin, they were strong, powerful women who put me to shame.

CHAPTER THIRTY-THREE

THE RIVER AND THE ROAD

On one of the first Sundays in Tengani, Gerard came early to prepare the small village chapel for Mass, as he was assigned to serve that small Catholic community. I was so grateful to see him; his masculine confidence and good humor comforted me at a time when I was still trying to find my feet on that new terrain.

His frequent visits allowed the "Tengani Three" to get to know him better. We discovered how much alike our thinking was on a wide range of topics that bubbled up over meals, prayer rituals, and shopping trips to Nsanje.

Gerard and I had an easy familiarity, but all three of us shared a warm camaraderie with him. He was one of those rare men who enjoyed women's company.

During the mass he introduced himself as the new itinerant pastor and the three of us as new neighbors. Afterwards, the parishioners came to our house to offer *Moni,* though they hesitated over how to address us; we were a new sight for most of them. Some called us *bambo* (man or father), since we were in Father Van Horne's house; some called us *dona* (lady); and for those who were Catholic, we were *mai sister* (mother or Mrs. Sister).

They pulled out rickety chairs for us and positioned them in front of our house. While the *kapitao* (elder) of the church played a drum, the children sang and two women handed us a small reed basket with three eggs. I hadn't expected such a formal program and was impressed that they thought to organize this official welcome.

I was sitting between Norma and Yoli and when the sweet program ended, and they both elbowed me to say our thanks, probably because I was the most outgoing—although my spoken Chichewa was the poorest. I'm not really certain what I said. I struggled to find the right words for thanks and to explain that we wanted to live in their village and learn from them. I hoped I didn't say anything offensive by a misspoken Chichewa word. The parishioners all laughed and clucked their tongues in delight over my childlike vocabulary and earnest effort.

Gerard smiled appreciatively at me from the edge of the crowd. When the formal ceremony ended with my little speech, he sought me out and shook my hand, an admiring look in his eyes. "Aimee, you did very well with your thanks to the parishioners. I was impressed. You have a warm way about you that the people see and feel—as I do."

I blushed at his words.

We mingled with the church community for a short time—what a curiosity we were to each other—and then the four of us squeezed into Gerard's tiny green car and headed for Nsanje to shop for sorely needed food and supplies.

A day or so later Sophia and Delia, who had been at the church welcome on Sunday, came to show us around the village. We stopped first at Sophia's hut, where she entertained us on her *konde*, constructed by supporting the extended thatched roofing with wooden poles.

Passersby could see us and crowded around, their heads poking under the thatch to offer the Asena greeting of *Botari* and get a closer look. I felt like a caged zoo animal on display and sympathized with those poor creatures.

Leaving there, the two women walked us to their nearby marsh gardens—their other field gardens lay miles away—and we picked our way through scratchy elephant grass to reach the snaking curve of the Shire River. Our first glimpse was of waves of colorful *nsaru* cloths, newly washed and draped atop bushes to dry. That was the women's section of the river.

Wanting to show us how they bathed, our two guides walked into the river, splashed water on their faces, and scrubbed their legs and arms with rough stones that they picked up from the shore. Then they scooped some mud with their fingers, rubbed it on their teeth, rinsed their mouths with the river water and drank a few gulps.

Nearby, skinny cattle waded haunch-deep, while women in knee-high water winnowed their baskets of grain. Others were bent over, beating their cloths on the rocks—which I tried doing—and bare-butted little ones played. An

elderly woman stood in the river shallows splashing water on her head.

Norma, Yoli, and I stared, jaws open, stunned by the complete disregard, or ignorance, of sanitation. I knew that the river teemed with bilharzia and other sickening organisms—not to mention the feces and urine added to the toxic mix. *How did they survive?*

My nursing education was getting kicked in the shins. That one image of the river was etched in my consciousness and helped me understand the colossal challenge of bringing modern medical care to Malawi.

That river, so central to their daily routines, their gardens, and fishing, would also flood with the January rains, isolating the villages from each other and washing away pieces of their already insufficient lives.

*

We accepted another invitation to tour the village with Elias, one of the village leaders, but we had no set time to meet him. No one had phones, watches, or clocks—the sun's position marked an approximate time. As one Malawian put it: "You Westerners are the slaves of time; we Africans, its masters." I stopped using my watch after my first week in Tengani. So we went to Elias' place during a free morning, hoping to find him. He wasn't at home but his wife provided us with chairs on their porch. We were quickly surrounded by squatting children with huge, staring eyes.

Elias soon appeared, dressed in a white robe and carrying a walking stick. He strutted among the huts with us in tow, proudly pointing out his trophy guests to everyone. He brought us to the medical assistant, who provided the most rudimentary care for Tengani and the surrounding area. We heard from others that he was often drunk and that his wife had accused him of adultery, so he had to go before the Nsanje court, missing days from his work.

We also learned from the medical assistant himself how frustrating his work was. The local Tengani villagers did not understand or appreciate his more Western approach and most often went to the medicine man for release from the evil spells and spirits they believed caused illness.

A few weeks later I returned to the medical assistant to discuss our tentative plans to do health teaching and get his advice. I was surprised to find him on the porch with his personal belongings packed: his chickens clucking in a crate, his mats rolled and tied, his few paper pictures down from the walls of his hut. He was leaving. He had asked for a transfer because, he said, "The people in Tengani aren't civilized." He was from another tribe and wanted to go further north to work "... and no, the government has not found anyone to replace me."

I worried what the community would do without any local medical help, especially after we left. We did tend to some of their minor problems and often drove our neighbors for medical care once we had the car.

Our little VW Beetle served as the village ambulance and taxi; we were often asked—or we offered—to take people to Nsanje, Blantyre, Muona hospital, or other distant villages for needed business or medical needs. Our Tengani teens always begged us for a ride anytime we got in the car—like typical teenagers everywhere. Though it was small, we always tried to load in any neighbor or stranger needing transport.

While that borrowed Volkswagen gave us much needed mobility—a great improvement over our bicycle—it also brought its own stressors. It frequently died on us during trips; the headlights failed, abandoning us to absolute blackness on two scary nights; and the tires often went flat. The only places for auto repairs were either in Nsanje or Blantyre, and we were right in the middle.

And driving was an adventure in itself.

On a six-hour trip to Phalombe for meetings, we were on one of the sharp bends of the escarpment when a tire went flat. A passenger we were bringing to the district hospital for a severely swollen foot got out with us to help change the tire, but we were on a slope and the car kept sliding backwards whenever we tried to jack it up. It didn't help that the jack was broken. Norma and I found big rocks to wedge behind the tires. Fortunately, some men walking down the mountain stopped to lend a hand, and we were on the road again in an hour.

On that same trip back, we had another mishap—a cow collision. The herder was frantically trying to move his languid cows off the road as we slowly approached, but one big gal in front hadn't gotten the message and sauntered into our path. When we parted after mutual profuse apologies, the herder's cow had a sore behind—and we had a smear of cowhide sticking to the fender.

*

Travel was often complicated by the sandstorms that blasted through the area in July and August. One storm began to stir the sandy landscape into a frenzy with pummeling winds just as we were returning to Tengani from a shopping trip to Nsanje. It was difficult to find the way to our house; we had to inch along in the car, ferreting out shapes as we wended our way through the village hoping not to hit any people, animals, or homes.

The sand stung our bodies as we raced from the car to the door of our house. Once inside, the sand blasted the windows and forced itself through numerous cracks in the walls. Its power to obliterate everything outside felt ominous. I wondered how our fellow villagers managed to come through the sandstorms when their fragile huts, their grazing animals, and their sparse clothing made them so vulnerable to nature's indifferent supremacy.

CHAPTER THIRTY-FOUR

THE OLD AND THE NEW

I had the opportunity to observe the medical assistant's competitor one afternoon when Norma and I went to a *madzoka*, a ritual performed by a *singanga* (native medicine man) wearing chains and crosses around his neck and a headdress that looked like that of a Catholic bishop.

Six old men were pounding on their skin drums as we arrived for the healing ceremony. The *singanga* cradled the sick girl in his arms and called on the evil spirits to leave her. The distressed family offered money to the healer and cups of *mowa*, which everyone then drank afterwards.

I was shaken by the eerie scene. The little girl was obviously very ill, and I had little hope that invocations alone would save her. Yet I couldn't intervene. I was witnessing the dearth of modern medical care in that obscure village, a mere speck on the map, she a mere sigh in the cycle of life.

At that time, I dismissed the medicine man's ritual as just a spectacle because his approach was so alien to my Western mindset. I did not yet understand the inherent cultural wisdom in indigenous healing practices and remedies.

The ceremony ended at dusk. We headed home, our band of followers growing. Parents, home from the fields, sat and watched our passing procession. We could never go anywhere without people, especially children, following us. I now knew what celebrities felt like—enjoying the popularity but longing to go about freely without an entourage.

Nearing our house, we came upon a young boy under a sausage tree, so called because of its long hanging fruit, playing the *ulimba*, a homemade instrument similar to a xylophone. Some of the children began to dance to the music and cajoled us to join them, which we did to their delight. I enjoyed the dancing, but soon we had to pull ourselves away from the group—night was encroaching and the mosquito squads were zooming in, searching for human blood.

A few days later in the dark before sunrise, the three of us responded to Chief Tengani's invitation and trekked to his hut. The chief and his three wives welcomed us with bottles of warm orange soda—ice was nonexistent. He had been in the Far East during World War II and his English was good enough for easy exchanges. He offered to show us his cotton fields.

The four of us were a strange group prowling the bush at dawn. Chief Tengani led us through tangled grasses to a wide stretch of cultivated rows of various plantings and offered us cotton samples to take home.

He was a funny-looking man, wrinkled and bent like a question mark. He wore an ankle-length skirt, misfitted spectacles on his nose, and he walked like a duck. When asked about his age, he said that he started working in 1913, so we guessed he might be in his seventies.

I was touched by his gracious openness to us, total strangers who had arrived uninvited in one of his villages. He seemed more educated than the people of his domain, and I liked his gentle, grandfatherly ways. Yet when the chief walked among his people they bowed and stepped aside to let him pass, demonstrating to us the importance of tribal authority. His power became obvious when he invited us to a meeting of all forty-two Lower Shire chiefs under him.

The gathering of the chiefs was held midday the next week. Elias came to escort us to Chief Tengani's hut, where we waited for the arrival of the government minister who would preside over the meeting. That provided us an opportunity to see the other side of the country's politics.

An hour later rhythmic drums called the people to the meeting underneath a gigantic jacaranda tree where the women were engaged in an energetic dance. Minutes later the minister arrived, dressed in a pressed blue shirt, slacks, and Hush Puppy shoes. He greeted all the chiefs and us—the honored guests—whom he was clearly shocked to see there. After avowals of support for President Kamuzu Banda by everyone, the minister began a speech that appeared to lack an end. The mosquitos had a field day; there were about two hundred edible people around, plus swarms of little children. Bitten unmercifully, we thought of leaving before the speech was over, but Elias, at our side, advised us not to—it would have been a sign of "despising." It was a stroke of luck that we heeded him, for a minute later the minister turned and pointed to us— the honored guests—sitting behind him.

His long-winded speech over, we lingered in the area and talked with the villagers who surrounded us. We were surprised when he sought us out to arrange a visit the next day.

Late the following morning the regional minister and his driver arrived in a Land Rover at our humble home. He clearly wanted to know what we were doing in the village. We were able to easily explain ourselves in English, and he seemed pleased by our desire to live and learn among his people. He himself was from the Lower Shire, though he now lived in Blantyre. When other missionaries later heard that the regional minister had visited us, they were stunned—he was a powerful figure in the Malawi Congress Party.

In one week we had witnessed a juxtaposition of the old traditional tribal system and the new face of the six-year-old government . . . and we had met a politician who would become a major player in the country's political history in subsequent years.

On a second visit to Chief Tengani's home, he invited us inside rather than sitting on the porch where he entertained most people.

He also came to visit us at our house one time and charmed us with the history of his chiefdom and more about his own life. When we went a last time to tell him we were leaving in a few days, he expressed sadness that we weren't staying, a regret I shared, as I would have liked to return and practice nursing among those wonderful people.

When we reached home after that first visit with the chief, the sun was still low on the horizon. Johan, some of our neighbors, and the usual bevy of children came rushing toward us, babbling about our being gone and how worried they all were when they came to our house early that morning and didn't find us there. I could see genuine concern and relief on their faces.

Anytime we left Tengani village for overnight trips, our return was met with a hero's welcome—the kids would come running alongside our car, shouting with delight, or jump up from our house steps, where they had been patiently waiting, their eyes widened in happiness. A few adults would soon appear offering us the typical greeting—shaking right hands, with their left hand lightly touching their right forearm. They questioned how we could go away without telling someone. A deep pleasure welled up in me to see how much we mattered to them. We had become members of the village.

CHAPTER THIRTY-FIVE

MVUU

In early August 1970 Yoli was called away to another assignment, leaving Norma and me alone in Tengani for the next two months. While Yoli had many of her own new experiences living in Blantyre, she missed the unending surprises Norma and I encountered after her departure, like our astounding exposure to an unexpected food source.

An urgent knock on our door brought a message that we must come to Ngona village immediately if we wanted to see the *mvuu*. That word was not in our vocabulary, but the insistent messenger made us feel we had to go. *Mvuu? What was that?*

We arrived breathless at my friend's hut in Ngona to discover that a *mvuu* was a hippopotamus—dead, not alive—lying in a section of the river that passed by their village.

Ena escorted Norma and me to the river bank, where we saw a gray, rounded mass on its side, two peg legs protruding from the water. A crowd of people had gathered. A hum of low voices filled the area like the seasonal swarms of flying ants.

A messenger had been sent to Nsanje government center—more than an hour's bike ride—to ask permission to use the carcass for meat, a rare commodity.

Another messenger had been sent to Chief Tengani to ask his permission.

On the sandy bank, groups of men huddled together, sharpening their machetes, which glinted in the hot midday sun. Women scurried to the site, ladened with reed baskets from their huts. Children raced along the water's edge, bursting with excitement. The expectant tension in the air captured and bewildered me.

The mood was palpable—hungry.

Finally the rider from Nsanje arrived, jumped off his bike and reported that the government said it would be unsafe to eat the hippo; no one knew why it died. It could be diseased. However, they deferred to Chief Tengani.

Now . . . more waiting.

Suddenly on the horizon, as in an old cowboy movie, we saw another man on a bike coming from the chief's house. He almost fell off it before it stopped, letting it clatter to the ground while shouting, "Chief Tengani said yes!"

The air became electric; everyone was instantly in motion. Brandishing their machetes, the men plunged into the river, the women anxiously clustered on the bank.

Without a word being spoken, as one body the men splashed toward the hippo carcass. One man cut off an ear, another the tail. These were then passed along the chain of villagers who stood in the water from the hippo to the bank. As a gesture of gratitude the token body parts were given to the courier, who jumped back on his bike to carry them to the chief.

Then, as if orchestrated, several men began hacking at different sections of the body. A sawed-off leg, chunks of skin and muscle, hanging entrails, and purple organs passed along the assembly line until they reached the river bank. As the minutes and hours passed, the dismembered hippo was piled high on the sand, forming a mound twice as large as the animal itself. I had to stand at a distance as flies swarmed over the raw flesh, which began to reek of decay in the scorching sun. Blood stained the sand, dripped off the hands of the men.

The river ran red.

The sun moved across the sky while Norma shot away with her camera and I stood transfixed and stared, repulsed—fascinated.

It took several exhausted men to roll the huge head onto the bank, their final effort after several hours of butchering. Only the bony skeleton was left to drift in the river's currents.

Then the women took over; the wives of the area chiefs had first pick, then the others came, baskets in hand, to claim a share of the mother-lode. Each took only small portions of the meat. No one rushed in to take more than the others.

I believe that the appearance of a dead hippo was unusual, so it was probably a startling experience not only for Norma and me, but also for the locals. Just as the episode remains vivid in my mind, I suspect it was a story passed down among the people to future generations. Perhaps, even today, some of them have heard of the Ngona *mvuu*.

Besides the exotic nature of the event, what stands in even stronger relief is the memory of a community—which never had much to eat—sharing in equal portions what was unexpectedly provided.

And some think them uncivilized.

CHAPTER THIRTY-SIX

HEARTLAND

One evening when the moon lit up the landscape, the teens came to fetch Norma and me for a neighborhood dance. When we arrived at an open expanse in the center of the village, mostly women and children with a few men were dancing with gusto to the beat of a big drum in the center of the circle. We were quickly surrounded by people wanting to greet us, offering their calloused hands to shake. Duly welcomed but feeling overwhelmed by all the attention—and choking on the stirred-up dust—we tried to slip away unobtrusively once attention returned to the dance. It was growing late and we were tired. Of course, it was obvious to everyone when we left.

The memory of a bonfire and wild drumming that seemed so frightening the night of my arrival in Tengani village, I now experienced as an enjoyable social event.

Moses and a few of his friends, our self-appointed guardians, walked us home—and terrorized us with dreadful stories of how a man hammered his wife to death the other night in a village a few miles from Tengani; how somebody else was boiled and eaten; how in 1967 two men were killed in the now vacant Tengani Indian store. They seemed to be vying to tell the most dreadful tale.

Before going to bed, we locked our windows and doors. That was the only time we did that, spooked by those eerie crimes told in the dark.

Other than that one night, an unspoken current of trust flowed between the local folks and myself. Many days I traveled alone through Tengani and surrounding villages. I'd meet someone along the way and they would invite me to visit their hut—and I would go, wanting to learn more about their lives, how they spent their time, how families managed. If I visited one home, the nearby neighbors would also expect a visit.

It was that way for all three, then the two, of us. We worked together much of the time, but each would go off alone to enter more deeply into the Malawian world—open to what would happen, what we would discover—choosing to be vulnerable in our solo explorations.

Early in September I visited a woman in another village. I intended to pay just a brief call. Our conversation turned into a meal together and introductions to her neighbors. So many hours had passed that a concerned Norma hopped in our car to search for me. A few minutes into her drive, she spied me on the road toward home, straddling the back fender of a wobbly bike and clinging to my friend's husband, the driver.

While I knew there was a dark underbelly to the culture, as with every culture, I never encountered unkindness from any Malawian in all my time there. I even had a proposal of marriage from a Tengani woman who thought I would make a good wife for her son.

The elemental realities of living in Tengani village stripped me down to a level of awareness previously inaccessible. I was only beginning to understand the truth of cultural adaptation and to glimpse the depth that it could take me. Immersion in another culture put in relief all the ways I still clung to my own cultural attitudes and behaviors, even though increasingly comfortable in my new environment. I was still far from getting inside their heads, their hearts.

Each person has their limit in adapting to another culture, but most of us don't begin to push against those boundaries. I noticed my own annoyance when people kept knocking at our door, repeatedly asking something from me, especially my time. I often craved solitude and time to read, study, and work on the assignments we had to complete for the Pilot Project.

Living in such a destitute environment was teaching me about my own coping abilities. The fact that I had taken a step inside village culture—

the reality for the 92% of all Malawians who don't live in towns—was opening mental doors for my future in the country.

These kind people were mired in a realism that I only glimpsed as a faint shadow: walking miles for clean water, having only fire to illuminate the dark, fearing illness and evil spirits with little to protect them against either danger. I watched them eke out a life—no, a survival—for themselves, their children, each day scrabbling together what they needed: kindling for the cooking fire, clothes to wear, seeds to grow, water to fetch, grasses to thatch their roof. They had no electricity or spigots in their huts, no mattresses, no regular income. The idea of comfort—even if sick, giving birth, or dying—was alien to them.

In spite of all that, the Malawians smiled and laughed readily, imparting the false impression that life was kind to them. They repaid their scarcity with an amazing generosity toward us, three white strangers who showed up one day in their midst.

Witnessing their lives, I became less and less focused on formal prayers or the Church's liturgy, which seemed foreign and out of place here. Most days, our shared morning and evening reflections were my prayer, along with simple Eucharistic services at our dining table when Gerard came, as priest and friend. The selflessness of being available to everyone became my prayer, my honoring of God by finding the Holy in each person, however ragged and ill—or wearing Hush Puppies.

I yearned to understand the meaning of my life in Malawi, and to surrender to all that was beyond my grasp.

An orthodox sense of "being a nun" was replaced by a gritty love and accessibility to these people who appeared so different from me. Yet in them I saw my parents worrying about the kids, my younger brothers and sisters wanting something more for themselves, moms loving their babies, old people wanting to talk, men relaxing with their beer. We shared that knot of relationships that made me feel akin to them. While exhausting me, my neighbors also surprised and delighted me. They made me want to know them at a deeper level, to socialize on their porches and to play with their kids—to be an equal, a peer in our shared personhood.

I was driven deeper into some heartland of humanity that made so much else inconsequential. In spite of the numerous burdens of each day—the heat and bugs, and the language difficulties—I had fallen in love with the people of *my* village.

*

In October 1970, a short time after I left Tengani and Father Van Horne returned to his little home from sabbatical, Gerard and a few of his fellow priests stopped in to welcome him back to the Lower Shire. Afterwards, Gerard wrote me:

> We stopped by Tengani—you remember that place—and Father Van Horne was telling us about "the sisters." The people in the village told him they had been very kind, maka-maka (especially) Sister Aimee, who they felt was chimodzi-modzi (just like) Father Van Horne, whom they love.

Gerard's letter pleased me. I was glad that my feelings for my neighbors were mutual.

CHAPTER THIRTY-SEVEN

GERARD

I was becoming aware of my attraction to Gerard as we spent more time together in Tengani and Nsanje. Besides his personal qualities of warmth, kindness, and humor that I admired, he was a virile man, at home in his athletic body. I always looked forward to his visits and thought that I maintained appropriate behavior around him, not considering that we had anything more than a good, meaningful friendship between a priest and a nun.

One August day weeks into our stay in Tengani, it was Norma's turn to write the day's summary in our communal logbook: "At midday, Gerard arrived on a bicycle all the way from Nsanje. His car was in the repair shop. He came with mail and to celebrate Mass for us."

Tucked under my mosquito net later that evening I penned a more intimate account:

> Gerard came today. He was terribly sunburned after biking more than an hour to reach us. Sweat made tiny worms in the dirt on his face and neck, and I wanted to pour cool water over his body. He was so exhausted from the ride and the heat but he was full of smiles when he greeted me.

In a subsequent letter Gerard admitted that, driven by his need to see me, he decided to bike to Tengani, ignoring the risks of long miles on a rugged road under a tropical sun.

Continuing my journaling the night of his quixotic bike ride, an unintended poem spilled onto my journal page:

I have dreamed in moments of awaking
Of being there to meet you, body-tired
And needing, at the door of our small world.
To smooth your brow and slip your tiredness off.
To curl about you like a lulling cloud,
That lifts you into a deserved peace
From a day long and well lived.
To say, with every inch of skin of me, that I care,
That I see the ache and long-leaning,
Want to make the distance shorter
by reaching out and into you.

Where had that poem come from? I didn't intend it to be about Gerard. I thought it only a poetic impulse prompted, perhaps, by his heroic bike ride.

How did I not realize what was occurring in me?

I remained in denial until one unforgettable day—September 14— toward the end of my stay in Tengani.

Norma and I, with Pieter and Gerard, took a day-trip by car to the Zambezi River. We were lucky to cross the border into Portuguese East Africa without any problems, though we had heard reports of it being risky to enter. After a brief visit to a missionary priest in Charré, who educated us about the tragic situation in that country strangled by oppressive Portuguese military control, we said good-bye to that lonely, despairing man. Sorrow about the suffering of the people weighed on our shoulders and cast a shadow on our sunny adventure.

Driving further south through a barren landscape as desolate as the Lower Shire, we reached the Zambezi River in an hour, got out of the car to stretch, and stood awestruck at the remarkable lattice-work bridge spanning it. We wanted to see more but were quite hungry, so we drove further on to the village of Mutarara, hoping to find some food. We had failed to bring anything, just assuming there would be a store in the town. We did find one, but the shelves were barren, and it appeared abandoned until a small Portuguese man hurried toward us from another room. He was clearly startled by the arrival of four strangers. When we motioned that we were looking for something to eat, the store owner gestured for us to wait, disappeared, and shortly escorted us to a back room where his family was eating. They had set another table. Though we could not speak their language to say what we wanted, they provided us with an amazing multi-course meal: soup, a meat stew, then steak and fried eggs. After that, another set of clean plates for papaya slices, then more plates for more fruit. We were disconcerted that they prepared it all just for us—the family had different, less generous amounts of food on their table.

As we began to push back out chairs to suggest we were ready to leave, little cups of espresso coffee were set before us. We thought we might have to wash the dishes for a month to pay for the meal, but it cost so little we felt embarrassed and gave the owner more than the number written on the torn piece of paper he handed us. Finally able to leave, we tried to show our appreciation to the gathered family in a shower of hand gestures and English and Chichewa. Though they couldn't understand our words we hoped they felt our gratitude.

Our bellies and hearts full from their overwhelming hospitality, we drove back to the striking Dona Ana Bridge, the longest railroad bridge in Africa, and walked halfway across it. Pieter clicked away with the camera, capturing Norma and me on the bridge.

The four of us then pushed a path through some tall grasses on the bank and sat on the edge of that historic river, fantasizing Livingstone's boats rowing by. Hunched beside each other, staring out at the water, Gerard's and my leg lightly touched.

Though we all wanted to linger and absorb the historic scenery, we returned to the car and raced to the border before it closed.

Back at the Nsanje mission house, Gerard and Pieter invited us for dinner. It had gotten dark and since our car headlights weren't working, it wasn't possible to return to Tengani. Norma and I accepted their offer to stay at the mission's guest quarters for the night, which we had occasionally done on earlier visits when daylight ran out before our long shopping list was completed.

The simple meal flowed into an evening of reflections on our incredible trip, along with our usual intense dialogues on missionary life, interspersed with rippling laughter. The hours evaporated. Finally Pieter retired and soon after, Norma—leaving Gerard and me alone.

Always the one to clean up, I started collecting the dishes and glasses that littered the sitting area to help Gerard bring them to a tiny closet-like space off the kitchen.

As I was placing the dirty dishes on the counter, I sensed Gerard behind me in the tight space, felt the heat from his body. Finishing my task, I turned to leave, but we were face to face, separated by only the thinnest layer of humid air. Stunned by our closeness, I faltered. Any words I might have said were stopped by Gerard's lips.

Our bodies blended easily against each other—a sensation for me that felt so new, so intimate, so unknowingly longed for. I stood wrapped in his strong arms with no desire to be released. Whatever appropriate resistance my brain tried to rally was short-circuited by the loss of any ties to reason. We clung to each other in a hungry, long-denied embrace that neither of us wanted to end. When we finally pulled apart, staring silently into each other's surprised eyes, I knew I had turned a fearsome corner with that shocking, delicious taste of surrender.

That kiss split me forever in two.

CHAPTER THIRTY-EIGHT

SLEEPLESS IN NSANJE

On September 16, 1970, Gerard wrote this letter:

My beloved Aimee,

It is Wednesday evening and I feel the need to write you about all what I felt since Monday night. I think that you, like me, very often went back to that wonderful moment, an unbelievable happening. It was the real expression of all what has been growing between us from the very first we met. I'm very grateful to you Aimee for this and I hope you have experienced it as something good, wonderful, precious.

Sometimes when I come back at that sacred spot in the kitchen I think of the moment I took your head in my hands, the moment that our both feelings came to expression in our first kiss. You said, "Gerard it is so nice to be loved." For me, it was the only way to express what was, and is, in my heart. The moment was even too short to express that, nevertheless, thank you for saying, "Gerard, let us go, otherwise they will find us still standing here tomorrow morning."

Walking you to your room it was full moon. I remember you said, "Our relationship has become very much deeper this evening." Yes, my dear, a kind of uncertainty about our feelings for each other has been removed. I think we should not be afraid to face the reality. I trust that we can expect from one another openness and frankness in our feelings, our problems. I didn't sleep that Monday night. I was just thinking, relaxed, lying on my bed smiling, wondering, not knowing what about, happy, uncertain, expecting. I thank you for all what

*happened since we met, and what the moment of Monday night
made possible.*

God bless you, my dear. I'm longing to see you soon.

Your Gerard

I hardly slept that night either—or the nights after. Though his kiss
broke open something tender and vulnerable in me, it also threw me
into tumultuous soul-wrestling beyond anything I had experienced until
then.

*What had I done? I had fallen into Alice's rabbit hole. Where was the
bottom to stop my fall?*

After that kiss in Nsanje, Gerard found his way to Tengani almost every
day. Heat waves rose off us like sunbaked clay whenever we were near
each other. While I endured an internal struggle with distressing yet
seductive emotions, Gerard continued to pen passionate letters.

18 September 1970

*My beloved Aimee, again I feel the need to write you about all what is
in my heart and mind, trying to make clear the complexity of feelings. It was so nice to see you yesterday when I came to say Mass at
Tengani, to feel your presence and warmth nearby.*

*I know one should not be lavish of love. For me, a personal relation-
ship to you is something holy. To kiss you, embrace you—all these
ways to express our feelings, doesn't come in one moment. I believe that
you and I are too serious, too honest for that.*

*I'm very eager to hear from you how you have experienced this. I hope
you are happy with our love. I realize quite well the difficulties caused
by it. In this sense it will make us more lonely. Yesterday alone in
your living room you whispered, "Gerard, our time becomes short." Yes
my dear Aimee, It will be terrible not to see each other frequently. I
told you already, every time I came to your Tengani house, it was as if
I came home. You were always there with a happy face, some cheerful
words to share with me.*

Our relationship which so wonderfully deepened this week, is not passing, not a caprice. However painful the distance between Phalombe and Nsanje may be, our hearts will be closely connected. I would be very pleased if we still found the possibility to talk before you are leaving. Let us not be afraid for the future. Let us feel free in our love, not too much determined by our surroundings.

My dear girl, I hope that God will help us. I pray for you. I know my prayer is very often poor and without words but a prayer from a warm heart must receive a warm welcome.

Aimee, strength and courage in these last difficult days before you leave Tengani. I think of you with grateful love and a sweet kiss on your lips.

Yours,
Gerard
"Many waters cannot quench love; neither can floods drown it."

How could I not be moved by a man of such sensitive passion, even though he had no idea of the profound split it caused within me: the magnetic pull of my religious commitment challenged by the opposing pull of a fire kindled in me, fanned by his love. Gerard's nurturance lifted me up—but guilt sucked me into the muck. I didn't know how "not to be too determined by our surroundings," as he advised in his letter. We were living in the midst of a conservative missionary subculture that would judge us harshly.

No copies of my letters to him remain; I have no memory of what I said in them, other than occasional lines Gerard quoted in his return correspondence. My letters were less frequent and rife with doubt and measured words of affection as I picked at my thoughts and feelings, like scabs on my skin. *What was I to do? How was I to understand what was happening to me?* It was more than I could attempt to find words for—or felt too ashamed—to put on paper.

CHAPTER THIRTY-NINE

SACRED VESSELS

On one of our last nights in Tengani, Norma and I invited Pieter and Gerard to a thank you dinner for all their support during our three months in the Lower Shire. Sitting across from each other in the tiny living room, Gerard's eyes and mine flashed at each other while the conversation flowed easily amongst the four of us good friends.

As the sun was dropping outside we ate the main course of chicken and rice, our serious reflections and ready laughter seasoning the simple meal. When night knocked at the windows, I went to get the pudding dessert I had prepared. Gerard offered to help.

The small kitchen was nearly dark. Finally alone, he reached for me with an intensity that had been building through dinner, impelled by the awareness that our time together was ending. He pulled me to him in a hungry embrace. Words of love and desire spilled from him as we kissed. Aware of our friends just a room away I felt reticent, but I couldn't resist. I felt consumed by him, by unknown physical sensations, as his hands and lips found my previously untouched breasts. The laws of gravity broke in me, sent me spiraling upward, downward, unbounded by all things rational, religious. Never had I felt such tender worship of my body. Gerard's embrace and fervent kisses slipped past my long-secured walls, eluded the guard dogs, and discovered, like Livingstone, an unvisited world within me. For the first time in my life, I knew my body as a sacred vessel.

I held his head, buried in my chest, and felt both treasured and frightened by what was unleashed. The tender words we murmured to each other were incoherent.

I finally pulled away, shaken by how I had surrendered to his caresses, and struggled to pull myself together. *How could this happen when I was a nun?*

We carried the awaited dessert to Pieter and Norma as though nothing had happened. They had to have known something was going on in that dark kitchen, hearing our sighs and whispers as they sat uncomfortably in the living room trying to make small talk. Yet I gave no thought to their suspicions when I returned. It was as though what was happening between Gerard and me occurred in some other ethereal realm disconnected from real life. In some unconscious way, some form of denial, I assumed that the ardor between us was invisible to others.

19 September 1970

Dearest Aimee,

What an evening yesterday! Unbelievable! Sorry darling that I didn't shave. I should've thought of that. I cannot believe that we could be so intimate last night in that small house with Norma and Pieter in the other room. The whole day today I was wondering that all these things happened in such a natural way. I don't know how to explain the last few days. I think there was already a long preparation for it. Both of us tried to hide it, but I think love is too strong to keep it hidden. I, at least, had to hide my feelings very consciously. Last night, in my room, I broke down for a moment, thinking of both of us in the future.

You said to me, "Gerard I don't know what happened to me. I have never had this experience, been so intimate before with someone. It is all new and unbelievable for me." Aimee, I felt the same.

I hope I haven't offended you because I'm always afraid to hurt your feelings. What exists between us is so precious that it gives us a great responsibility for one another; you are not anymore on your own. That makes love so really unselfish but also difficult.

I send this letter by Pieter. I told him there is an article for you, and I found an article to include, but that is just packing. I'm longing for you darling. Believe me, you are no moment out of my mind.

Aimee, my beloved, God help us.

Gerard   (sorry for my English mistakes)

He continued to honestly expose his feelings in letters, while I seemed to deny what was happening between us until one night when I finally confronted myself in my journal:

So here I am in an intimate relationship with a man for the first time in my twenty-seven years! How can I think about this clearly? Tengani has made me aware of a need for a man in a way I never considered before. I find myself wanting to abandon myself to Gerard and it scares me that I feel all reserve dissolving. I am afraid of losing my self; I never wanted to give my all to any one or anything other than God.

Gerard is so confident about our relationship, our compatibility, while I still linger in disbelief that I could be loved just as I am. While I am comfortable with emotional connections, I am uncomfortable—inexperienced—with physical intimacy. What am I to think, what am I to do? I need time away to think this out. Perhaps when I return to Phalombe . . . or to Likuni for the tropical medicine course.

That need for emotional isolation reflected my childhood belief that I had to figure things out on my own. Never during the confusing weeks and months that followed did I ask anyone for counsel or seek advice from an older, wiser person—perhaps because I felt there was no one I could trust to understand my dilemma.

And God and the saints weren't speaking to me anymore.

On our last full day in Tengani before we had to return north to Phalombe over the Cholo escarpment for what, I thought, would be my last time, Norma and I sat on the steps of our little home, looking up at the southern constellations and a clear moon smiling down on us.

Africa's nights were typically so densely black they were frightening; several times we had been caught out in them and couldn't see our hands in front of us. I didn't fear what might be lurking in the dark, but the dark itself. It was so absolute.

Many weeks earlier after a prolonged visit with the medical assistant on the far side of Tengani, we realized dusk had passed while we sat inside his clinic. It was pitch black as we started walking home. We had traveled across the world but couldn't find our way in our own village. We kept shouting *Moni* and *Njira ku nyumba kwathu iri kuti?* (Where is the way to our house?). We were laughingly rescued by a woman neighbor and her curious children who came out of their hut and took each of us by the hand. We walked to our house, led along like blind people. Our rescuers were able to see through the wall of night, while our sight could not penetrate it.

When one hears an answering *Moni* in the dark from unseen lips, one can't help but acknowledge that what is essential is invisible to the eye.

But that last night, for the two of us on the steps, the planets shone in all their cloudless beauty, adding to our bittersweet awareness that our sojourn in Tengani was over.

After Yoli's departure at the end of the first month left us a twosome, Norma and I had become close friends, enduring challenges and celebrating discoveries unimagined before we arrived in that nowhere village. We were tested and came out stronger, had amassed solid insights and appreciations for the culture, and had made friends with those kind people. We also hoped we had made some positive contribution. Besides our daily ministrations to our neighbors, we had taught many of the children the mystery of reading and writing the alphabet and spelling their names, taught nutrition and health lessons to the teens and women, and used our influence to bring a new medical assistant and community worker to Tengani.

However, more than any of those small offerings, I believe the greatest gift we gave—and received—was a sense of mutual respect. We were the new brand of missionary, come to share the Gospel's Good News that we are all equal in our common humanity.

As it was late, Norma went inside but I lingered on the steps, unwilling to let go of the magical night around me, resistant to ending it, for then tomorrow would arrive—my last day with the people of Tengani and Gerard.

CHAPTER FORTY

LIKUNI TROPICAL MEDICINE COURSE

Norma and I safely reached Phalombe after the arduous trip from Tengani over the Cholo escarpment. It was a melancholy journey for me.

We only had two days to unpack and repack for a week-long tropical medicine course. In that short time home, the sisters seemed to treat us with a new respect since we had lived in a village for three months in the poorest region of the country—an accomplishment none of them had achieved. Yet the memory of my frustrations during those first months in that Phalombe community left me uncertain of my place among them. My hope was that I could gain a foothold, some genuine acceptance by the sisters once I was familiar with tropical diseases and could demonstrate my professional nursing skills. The sisters in Phalombe focused on work to the near exclusion of everything else. Perhaps assisting in the hospital would be my entrée into their circle.

But being in the midst of that large community of religious women created a new dissonance for me after discovering myself as a sexual woman. I felt different, apart, and ashamed to talk about my divided affections with anyone, even Norma. Only since the writing of this have I learned from the others in the Pilot Project that they had observed the undeniable attraction between Gerard and me from the first days of our Likulezi course—but had kept their silence.

Though far away from him, our relationship was ever present in my mind. It had complicated my life, shaken its foundations. I knew he loved me; he had even mentioned marriage, but I was lagging far behind. My commitment as a Medical Mission Sister was still such an integral part of my identity. I cared deeply—at a soul level—for Gerard, but was what I felt *Love?* The unmasking of my sexuality had distorted my sense of direction, as in the childhood Pin the Tail on the Donkey game when one is spun in circles.

Added to all this I was battling a bone-deep fatigue. Once away from Tengani, my body let me know how exhausting those three months had been. Perhaps the different setting of Likuni would give me time for rest—and distance to think more clearly about my situation.

In a September 29, 1970, letter to my parents, I described my latest location:

> I'm writing this letter in an inner courtyard with riotous shades of bougainvilleas spilling over my shoulder. It's dusk, and a cool wind is blowing away the sticky heat of midday. Farther south in Tengani and Nsanje, it's unmercifully hot, as it's now the dry season, but mornings and evenings are crisp and breezy here in the central region.

> Two days ago we traveled from Phalombe, north through Zomba, Dedza, finally reaching Likuni, about five miles outside the "big city" of Lilongwe. Several of us from Phalombe Hospital are attending a five-day tropical medicine course along with twelve other expatriates and Malawians. We have four classes each day and observation time in the hospital.

> The program focuses on the treatment of village medical conditions when there is no hospital facility nearby—which is the situation in most of Malawi. The lack of physicians in the country requires nurses and other health assistants to assume many of the functions normally done by doctors at home. I'm deluged with new terms and procedures; realize what a long way I have to go to become competent in tropical nursing.

I felt as if I were continually in the role of student in every aspect of my life: sorting through a relationship with a man, finding my place within the three different languages and cultures in my own Phalombe community, wading into Malawian culture and its multiple dialects—learning to care for the ill and destitute in a medical environment that was altogether foreign. I longed to feel at least professionally competent—to have some solid ground on which to stand.

In my journal a couple of days later, I wrote:

> Here I am at Likuni trying to do wise thinking between lectures. The program is intense, and I worry about my lack of knowledge and skills. My few months in a Philadelphia hospital after graduation hardly gave me enough practical experience for an easy transition into what is demanded here in Malawi.
>
> I'm in a state of continuous fatigue and low enthusiasm, and I don't know the cause. Is it the ongoing adjustment to the culture? A sub-clinical illness? Disillusionment with the colonialist missionary mentality...or some truths needing to be confronted? I feel like the new girl on the playground, standing on the sidelines, waiting for an invitation and the right angle of the jump rope to join in.
>
> I've become too undisciplined these days—can't say no to an offered cigarette, can't concentrate, can't sleep, can't even seem to pray. I think only of myself and my struggles. Where is my willpower? My ability to manage my life, to see all the good around me? I fear I am losing something so central—my ability to put the needs of others first.

I wrote to Gerard expressing my distress. He responded promptly.

My dearest Aimee,

Your feelings of professional dissatisfaction are quite understandable. You need to be able to practice your profession, and test your ideas about health care that you have shared with me.

About your discontent and disillusionment—you know I think you got a shock by the experiences here, and not only culture shock. I think your life was too safe, too sweet and maybe too idealistic, Aimee, and so perhaps a bit unrealistic. In the beginning of our course at Likulezi, I have often felt surprise to listen to you talk about your ideals for work in Malawi. I came much more uncertain, without high expectations—and even for me it is not easy to handle the situation here. So, I can a bit imagine how hard it is for you. You are in heart a cheerful, happy person. Please don't lose yourself. Maybe you have come nearer to the reality of life. Your questions about the Church and religious life are mine as well, already for a long time. I feel too much the legalism in the Church, too less the incarnation of the message of love and Christian freedom.

Aimee, you wrote: "Don't love me too much, Gerard." This was hard to understand, but I know that everything is too uncertain, and sometime I wonder if I was right to express my love that night in Nsanje, but it just happened, unplanned. Maybe my love is too much for the moment? Still, I think it is strong enough to move slow together with you. I know that you love me, as I love you, and that the other values you hold are still so influential in your life. Time will show us which way we have to go. I know that there will still be troubled times, but I hope our love is bigger than our fear.

As you said in your letter, I too look forward for the day that our paths will next cross. I don't feel afraid at all, but I understand your mixture of fear and excitement for our next meeting in late October. Don't be afraid too much, Aimee, I am with you in a slow-motion love,

Gerard.

How could he always be so confident about us? I longed to have his certainty, but he was older and had begun to question his vocation while still in the Netherlands. While Gerard spoke often of how much he loved his priestly work with people, he had come to realize that his character was not well suited to celibacy, nor to the solitude he endured in isolated Nsanje. Gerard was a social man who thrived among people. One of many young boys who entered the minor seminary at fourteen, he had not experienced enough of life to know who he was. Even as he entered his twenties, it was within the confining requirements of the priesthood. While he was not supported in his expressed opinions about priestly celibacy among the missionaries with whom he worked, Gerard was not alone in his desire for the option of a married priesthood. I shared that view then, as many do today.

In touching letters, Gerard told me of his longing to have a wife, home, and children. That desire had surfaced in him well before we met, and he believed he had found in me his ideal partner.

It was different for me. Ever since I was a young girl, I had eschewed marriage and having children. They were not what I envisioned for myself. I enjoyed living in community with other women—at least back in the States—and doing the international healing work of a Medical Mission Sister. As compatible as our personalities were in so many ways, there was a deep gap between Gerard and me in the matter of marriage. His increasing reference to it in the coming months, and the appeal of working together in Malawi, was cracking open my defenses on the subject. At the same time I felt an undercurrent of pressure from the discrepancy between his repeated hopes and my readiness. Pulled between two divergent sets of values and lacking a certain maturity, I was unable to express, even to myself, how radical it was for me to consider marrying anyone. For Gerard, the magnetic attraction and sweet intimacy between us was normal, natural, comfortable—while I banged and bumped around in my thoughts, unable to find my true north.

Clearly, I needed more time to honestly work through my dilemma and reach a decision. But that time would be denied me.

CHAPTER FORTY-ONE

OASIS

The change of settings over the past few months—Phalombe, Muloza, Tengani, then Likuni—left me confused, not only as to the correct day or date in my journals, but also where I was in my inner landscape.

There was still one more place to go before I would finally settle in Phalombe and assume my role as a nurse in our hospital. The program planners understood that the five of us in the Pilot Project would need some R&R after such a demanding program of cultural adjustment and study. We arranged to go to Lake Malawi, 350 miles of deep water running north and south along the eastern border of the country. The lake was created by the splitting of the African tectonic plates—the great Rift Valley.

In mid-October, Pat, Norma, Yoli, Flora, and I loaded into the only vehicle large enough to transport all of us: our rusty, trusty ambulance. It was a typical vehicle in that it had no windows in the back cab and only two parallel benches on the sides—so we took turns sitting up front or on the benches. I didn't care how rough and jarring the long ride north was; the image of a shimmering lake pulled me forward like an oasis in the desert.

Passing signs that read "Elephants have right of way," we bumped and jostled on washboard roads for six hours until we reached the southern tip of the lake, between Monkey Bay and Fort Johnston. Arriving at our rental home felt like finding solid ground after being at sea.

The area where we stayed was populated by troops of baboons that ran across the roadways and clamored on our house roof, their babies astride the mothers' backs. The sky hosted vibrant-hued parakeets and eagles, whose screeching cry raised my skin hairs. Grunting, tank-like hippos wallowed near white storks as still as statuary in the lake's lagoons. It felt like a jungle paradise.

Our rented house was right on the lake, its large glass windows looking out at cerulean water that stretched to the misty mountains of Portuguese Territory on the far horizon.

My mind arrived weighted down with issues: Gerard, concerns about my reentry into the Phalombe community, and the hospital work awaiting me. But once I emptied my suitcase and settled into our rustic lake house, I unpacked my mind as well. I desperately needed not to think for a while, not even about Gerard. My only desire was to sleep for a month in the eight days I had.

I could usually be found cradled in a beach hammock under a palm tree or floating in the sultry waters. Through heavy lids, I watched fishermen

in dugout canoes slipping their wood paddles in—and—out, in . . . and . . . out. At times, a languid smile slid across my face at children's laughter further up the beach. I thought about nothing but where the sun was in the sky, how many pages were left in my book, *Livingstone's Lake,* or whether I was hungry.

A few adventures did spark me back to life after hours vegetating under the rustling palm fronds.

One cooler afternoon I meandered up the beach and perched on a jumbled pile of rocks at the lake's edge. After staring at the horizon for a long time, I glanced down toward my legs and was startled to see a snake protruding from a nearby crevice. I was about to bolt when a closer look showed it to be only a shed skin. Thinking it would be a neat souvenir, I started pulling on it, never thinking that the snake might still be attached at the other end. Fortunately it wasn't, though it was probably curled up inside those rocks. Walking back home with my four-foot papery treasure dangling from my hand, a passing boy said it was the skin of a forest cobra—one of Africa's most aggressive and venomous snakes. *Yikes!*

On another afternoon, Pat and I hiked a densely forested hill and chanced on a panoramic view of the lake. We stood in awed silence, absorbing the spectacular scenery, all the more exquisite as the dipping sun burnished land and water into gold leaf. Though we didn't want to end the magical vision, we knew we had to return before we lost daylight. Starting to walk down from our perch on the hilltop, several yards away we noticed what appeared to be a human skull . . . and then another . . . then some long bones . . . a humerus . . . a tibia.

Dear God, what had we come upon?

Recalling that the baboons came from that direction, we concluded that it was their burial ground. After exploring the area we felt a bit spooked and scurried back down the hill, leaving their sacred spot to them.

Midway through our stay, the five of us made a foray to buy groceries in the nearby town of Monkey Bay and decided to see more while we were out—and while I was upright. We drove further on to Cape McClear, a stunning point on a nub of land jutting out into the lake. After the desert environment in Tengani, to be surrounded by water on three sides was liquid heaven.

We followed a sign to Old Livingstonia, the first settlement of missionaries to arrive in the wake of the famed explorer who had reached that spot in 1859. It was constructed as a physical and spiritual fortress to interrupt the slave routes.

Only a few crumbling buildings remained, overtaken by possessive vines. A crude sign pointed to a burial site, so we left our car and walked a good distance into the bush. We almost fell over five weathered crosses, tipped over by time's careless hand. They marked the deaths of a few of the many settlers who died from malaria in the 1880s.

The poignant sight prompted the first serious thought of my holiday. They were missionaries, like me, yet of a different religious and cultural mentality, shaped by a different time in history. While I honored their self-sacrifice, I wondered if they had any positive or enduring effects on the local people. Were they directly involved in stopping the thriving, inhumane slave trade, or just seeking converts? Was the loss of their own country and the deprivations they endured worth it? What remained of their sacrifice and efforts, other than those five forgotten crosses?

And what would remain of mine?

CHAPTER FORTY-TWO

HOSPITAL CALLS

Rested from my lake holiday, I returned to Phalombe. It wasn't long before the pressures and tensions returned. The large and disparate community felt constraining after the intensity and independence of village life those previous months. Still, I committed myself to reengaging with the Dutch sisters and, though anxious about my new role, began working in the hospital.

My relationship with Gerard continued to take a back seat in my thoughts, pushed aside by the more immediate challenges confronting me. They required all my mental energy.

My hospital exposure began with night duty, anticipated to be an easier transition since that shift was usually the quietest; most of the patients were sleeping. Unlike in America, we didn't take vital signs every four hours. A student nurse circulated through the hospital to alert me if there were any problems. Lying in the small bedroom off one of the wards, I could hardly sleep for dread of what unknowns I, an inexperienced nurse, might have to deal with. I was the only RN on duty in the entire hospital.

Midway between dusk and dawn my first night, a man was lugged in by several others, his unsupported bloody limbs dangling. He writhed in pain from violent machete wounds. His bearers plopped him on a hallway gurney—and left. *God, help me!*

The only light I had to examine him by was a kerosene lamp swinging from the raised arm of the equally nervous student. The man needed an intravenous line started and preparation for surgery before the doctor would be called. The swaying lamp waved shadows on the man's arm.

In the near dark, I palpated for a vein hidden beneath his black skin. My hands shook. After three failed tries, I became panicky—*how was I supposed to do this in the dark?* I'd had minimal experience starting IVs in nursing school; that was the job of trained technicians. Frantic, on the brink of swearing and deeply worried about the patient, I entreated the student to go for the matron, who arrived ten minutes later, reeking annoyance at being awakened. While she inserted the needle with relative ease, honed from years of experience, she berated me for needing to call her for help. I clearly hadn't passed muster.

Crushed that I failed to prove myself capable, I knew the story of my incompetence would quickly spread among the sisters the next day. I could see the shake of their heads, hear their *tsk, tsk* at my lack of skill.

The hospital was quiet on my remaining nights, allowing me to sleep until morning and wake feeling relief. Yet it also deprived me of a chance to show I could handle other situations that might occur.

From early November 1970 until mid-March of 1971 my work in the hospital gave shape to my days. With greater confidence I was doing occasional night shifts and covered some of the wards during days when other sisters needed help.

Night duty at the hospital became less of a concern after that initial and humiliating trial by fire. The hospital was usually quiet once dark fell, and I was familiar with the routine. Before I retired I walked through the wards to see that everyone was settled: patients asleep in their beds, family members lying on the floor by them. I was always grateful when I woke after an undisturbed night to the low hum of voices and the stirring of patients and their families outside my little room.

A new level of responsibility came after a week of apprenticeship in the outpatient department (OPD), where I learned how to diagnose and prescribe for the most endemic conditions. Still a neophyte, I soon became the nursing supervisor of that department.

I worked six days a week in outpatient care from seven-thirty a.m. until two p.m. and returned in the late afternoons as needed. Norma and I shared responsibility for the department, and we loved working together.

The OPD, in one end of the hospital, consisted of a large room where we assessed and treated patients, and a few smaller rooms for eye and wound care and minor surgeries. One young man registered the patients at the outside window and accepted their few pennies of payment. Another worked inside, applying dressings and dispensing medicines. With the translation assistance of the student nurses, I did intake on each one, listened to their complaints, and prescribed and treated them unless they needed to be referred to Norma. We saw between 150 and 200 people each day.

While I loved working with the patients and Malawian staff, it was intensely challenging to conduct my interviews in Chichewa and to work with such limited equipment. We had to reuse the needles, which lost their fine edge and became jagged. Giving an injection through the sun-toughened skin of an African with a dull, barbed needle required me to lean all my body weight to push the syringe into the muscle. I hated having to do that, but the patients never complained.

Some of my most satisfying months in Malawi were working in the OPD. Norma and I, along with the rest of our Malawian staff, functioned as a team, an alien concept to the Dutch hospital model, where each sister's department or ward was her turf.

Noting that the patients usually waited for hours, squished together on the long benches in the open room, I suggested the nursing students teach our captive audience basic health and hygiene practices and answer their general questions. This allowed Norma and me to spend more time with each sick adult or worried mother. Neither she nor I believed in treating people as if they were on an assembly line.

The hospital matron occasionally observed in the OPD, poking her nose into everything and looking over my shoulder as I prescribed. I found her behavior annoying. She complained to other sisters that Norma and I took too much time with the patients—reminiscent of my student hospital days—but I knew we were making a difference. The student nurses confided to Flora how much they enjoyed working with Norma and me.

My sense that we were on the right course was strengthened when the catechists at Likulezi told me that their wives liked to come to the outpatient department after Norma and I were there. One of them wrote to me after I was gone:

> Our women are complaining for you very much because of the hospitality you did at Holy Family Hospital. When you were there, they were very happy because they met their best friend who could serve them with no hesitation.

Norma and I were building meaningful links between the people and the hospital, caring for everyone who came, never turning anyone away, even if it meant we occasionally came late for meals—another source of criticism from the other sisters.

I couldn't win.

Though busy with the OPD, night duty, and occasional ward coverage, I was pleased to be asked to help teach first-aid to the students at Likulezi. It allowed me to get off the compound and freely interact with the Malawian catechists training at the Center. I enjoyed those male students because they all laughed at my jokes and my misspoken Chichewa. I tried to teach in their tongue and they coached me when I didn't know some of the technical terms.

When the time came for me to leave for a new assignment in March 1971, the men begged to sing and dance for me as a good-bye gift. Once outside, they pulled out their drums and called for their wives to join them. The men began dancing in a circle, bells strapped to their ankles or seed pod rattles in their hands, while others drummed. The women sat on the ground, babies in their laps, clapping and making unusual rhythmic noises with their mouths, sounds I could never reproduce.

When the impromptu program ended I began my rounds, shaking each person's hand, saying over and over: *Zikomo kwambiri* (thank you so much) and *Tsalani bwino* (good-bye).

One man held my hand in his and asked, "Why are you leaving, instead of those other sisters, when you belong here with us?"

And another: "We see how you love us, love the Malawians that you meet and work with here. We don't want you to leave. You are different from the other sisters."

Their words lingered in my heart as I pedaled my way back home to Phalombe, carrying gifts of carrots and a candle. I did feel a love for them— they were my people.

CHAPTER FORTY-THREE

THE CLEAVING

The Malawians did indeed feel more like my people than my own sisters. In spite of repeated efforts, I couldn't find the key to gain their acceptance, especially from the leadership of the community and the hospital. A handful of dominant personalities directed and decided everything, with little influence from the remaining sisters. It felt that my efforts and actions were met by either overt or hidden criticism. One sister reported me to the executive committee for wearing my *nsaru* as a skirt on my days off.

My journal entries during those months in Phalombe—the last quarter of 1970 and first months of 1971—were filled with discouragement, even hints of depression:

> Phalombe has killed my joy in community by so limiting the possibilities of each individual. The authoritarian structure grinds in upon itself. Maybe I could help these women if they didn't inhibit my own energy so much. I'm emotionally consumed by internal conflicts among the sisters—and with me. Perhaps I could be more at peace in another MMS community— but where could I go? I don't want to leave Malawi.

*

> I have the vague feeling of trying to put a puzzle together with a central piece missing. It's as though I'm standing on the outside of all my interactions—distant,

not involved in what I'm doing except when I'm working with the patients and families in the hospital.

A storm has been brewing all day since I got up, and it broke this evening in drenching tears. We had a community meeting with our district superior, who continues to be very critical of the Pilot Project, and I made several cynical remarks. What is happening? This isn't me. At supper, I ate in silence and went to the chapel to pray but cried instead. I feel so alone in this community. I need to feel loved—or at least liked—to be able to be loving. Perhaps it is a weakness in me; a Christian should love without return—but I'm not sure I can do that. I am happiest and at my best when I can be loving and giving. Can I love without being loved? Will it strengthen ... or destroy me?

When a visiting American MMS from Uganda was leaving Phalombe for the airport, she pulled me aside. "Aimee, I fear you have a lonely year ahead; you have given so much but have gotten so little support." It was a sad comfort to have her confirm my own feelings.

While my community was wearing me down, Gerard tried to build me up. His frequent letters, full of assurances of his love, piled up on my desk. I couldn't write him often enough, disappointing that lonely man far south in sweltering Nsanje. Gerard lived with one unsocial fellow priest, so he suffered from a lack of companionship, but he didn't have the demands on his time and energy that I did in a group of almost thirty sisters. I felt increasingly guilty that I wasn't keeping up with his letters, didn't as easily express my feelings of love back to him, wasn't able to make our relationship the priority that it was for him. Not that I didn't want to; I was unable to juggle all the rings tossing in the air. Doubts about my ability to be his equal, the friend and lover he longed for, dampened my expectation of what was possible between us. I felt I was the weaker, less loving person.

Once I left Tengani in September 1970, letters between us were our only link; we spoke of our mutual anticipation of seeing each other again at the seminar scheduled for late October. Gerard also often mentioned his distress driving past a certain vacant house on his many trips around the Lower Shire:

> *Yesterday I passed Tengani shortly after sunrise and felt the strong inclination to bang on your door, enter your room, and kiss you good morning . . . but you weren't there.*

Back on the Phalombe compound, I wrote him of my fears about how our relationship would be perceived by the sisters if they found out. He wrote back:

> *I thought over and over again about your words, and I found myself with tears in my eyes because I feel so unmighty, so paralyzed. I feel angry that such a beautiful thing as our love is not allowed to grow and come alive. I pray for you and us, not in a formalistic way, but in a personal way, a mixture of praying and protest, love and longing. I hope we shall find the way to be happy.*

*

In the waning days of October 1970 Norma and I scaled back our work at the OPD so we could attend the afternoon seminar at Likulezi with our teacher, Father Prinsen, and all our former classmates.

Gerard came to Phalombe on Monday morning before the first session and wrote later about his anticipation of our reunion:

> *I was so nervous and excited that I drove to Phalombe from Blantyre in under an hour, too quickly, but love gives wings. I was all the way wondering, "How will she be? Shall I see her today? Who is she, really?" After four and a half weeks, it looks like you are going to meet a new person. So, our first meeting at your house on Monday morning before you went to the hospital was full of trembling uncertainty. Then you smiled and said, "Gerard, it is so good to have you near." The uncertainty left me; "She is still alive, she still loves me."*

I was glad to see him; his solid presence calmed me, but it also stirred up my anxiety of being seen with him. A long month had elapsed before the seminar brought us back together, but we were surrounded by classmates and we had little private time to meet.

The seminar focused on our research projects of the past few months and how our Chichewa was progressing. It was exciting to hear everyone's account of the many new and positive experiences with the Malawians, but discouraging to hear about the confrontations our group continued to have with the missionary subculture in which we had to function.

Gerard and I usually sat beside each other in the arc of desks and chairs. Sometimes his knee or my elbow found the other. We socialized with everyone during the breaks, but there was a gravitational pull between us. If they hadn't seen it before, our classmates and the Phalombe sisters must have observed the unmistakable spark that flew between Gerard and me, even though I thought we were being discreet.

I was blind—to so many things.

October 26, 1970, journal:

> Today, at our first session, it was difficult to be so close yet have no chance to be alone with Gerard. We don't know when we might see each other again after these brief four days.
>
> This is such a bittersweet experience. Gerard is so good, so sensitive a man, and our personalities fit so easily together, almost mirror each other. Yet the situation of our religious vows and communities gives us no space, no time to evaluate what is between us. I feel a crack growing inside me—I am a woman with two conflicting loves. I can only try to be honest with myself and hope for some light as I go step by step through this. I feel the heaviness of my responsibility right now; my decision could affect so many others.

Over the next three days of the seminar, Gerard came to see me in the mornings in the OPD or in the evenings in our communal living room with the other sisters present. He was the only one of the male classmates at the seminar who visited so often, lingered so long. How obvious he was in seeking me out; how uncomfortable I was with that public exposure.

As a man, Gerard possessed a natural balance of tender concern and poetic passion, what I now know to be a rare blend. As a priest, he'd recognized that celibacy was not a healthy fit for him and was honestly trying to find his way through the incongruity of our situation. He knew I needed time, without pressure, before I could make any decision, but it seemed impossible to find that elusive elixir.

The last night of the seminar, knowing he would be leaving the next morning and with no sense of when we would meet again, Gerard came after midnight, tapping on my bedroom window. It was a shocking thing to do; there were other sisters sleeping in the house, and neighbors only a stone's throw away. Earlier that day, he whispered of coming to see me and I protested: "Gerard, that would be unwise, unsafe for you to come. We can't, we shouldn't." But I caved to his entreaties, placing the need for a last time to be with each other over my need to avoid such a risky venture.

We had one short hour together.

As soon as he was back in Nsanje, Gerard wrote in praise of that night:

When I entered your room that last evening, we stood quietly inside your door and you laid your head on my shoulder and poured out your feelings. It was so nice to hold you, give you some protection with my arms, and listen, like a husband coming home from work and hearing about your day. I tried to say with my kisses how beautiful you are to me. I hope that you feel that.

Aimee, our time together was redemption after the long weeks apart. I'm still a bit intoxicated. You have been so good for me. I'll never forget that. I felt a kind of sorrow when I arrived, for I knew that I would have to leave—for maybe a long time. I felt tears come as I whispered good-bye.

I think it was good for our relationship and understanding of each other to have had that private time together. Don't you think so?

Did I think so?

What would I have said if I had had the words that night?

I am a mountain climber—my feet straddling a running crack in the ice.

I am a sailor—one foot on the dock, the other on the prow of a boat pulling away.

I am a woman split in two by human love—and the fear of its consequences.

How could I describe the desire he lit in me by his presence in my bedroom, by the heat of his body stretched beside mine—yet having my fears douse my passion—fear of intimacy's possible aftermath for me as a woman . . . and of the judging eyes of heaven for me as a nun.

Though our brief time together was full of whispered words and newfound pleasures in each other, we denied ourselves the ultimate union, even as our bodies longed for it.

In the following days, a voice in my head castigated me for that hidden hour together. I had allowed a man into my room and had savored our sweet intimacy. The voice berated me—it was all my fault—I had let down the veil.

Guilt became my daily companion.

Is it ever possible for any man, even one as sensitive as Gerard, to understand that sexuality for most women is never simple? For me—unable to ignore my vocation and sensitive to the criticism of my community—it couldn't have been more complicated.

I knew other priests and sisters had made clear, easy decisions to leave religious life when they discovered a personal love. There was no clarity, no ease for me. Was it because I didn't love Gerard enough? Or loved my vocation more? Was I afraid of surrendering to human love? Or of dealing with all that would fall apart in my life if I chose him?

I resolved that I would no longer meet Gerard in secret. I felt I was living a lie . . . but his love, conveyed in letters and messages through a mutual friend, was so real. Someone valued me, saw all that I wanted to give. The taste of human love made my celibate life seem rigid and lonely.

But I did meet him again. I could not resist Gerard. When I was in his presence, he was a magnet, I the scattered iron filings unable to pull away from him—though I always would, in the end. It was always me who pulled away. While I wanted to please him, wanted to be the woman he invited me to be, I had no sense of a healthy sexuality or of the personal autonomy needed when a decision begged to be made.

When Gerard was absent, I was wholly immersed in the medical work I had been drawn to and enjoyed pouring out my life for the Malawian people, whom I also loved.

When I was among my sisters, I tried to pray and connect and work alongside them, but their world was so different from mine, and we were never at home with each other. Those days I found myself increasingly looking at religious life from the outside. Before, I had been so inside it I couldn't see any other angle. Now I felt that who I appeared to be and who I really was, were two different people.

I was at home with Gerard, especially when all the other rings I tried to keep in the air slipped out of my hands, if only for fleeting moments. We shared a desire to work together with the Malawians as equals and to explore what it meant to be fully human, fully loving, but we were caught in a Catholic missionary culture that didn't understand that new theology—or us. We tried to be honest about the vows we had both taken—and were breaking by our relationship—and we wanted to find a way to get clear and straight with ourselves, our communities, and God.

I ached to tell someone of the demons that chewed at my spirit; that made me feel bad even though something, somewhere in the depth of it all, felt good and true.

Unable to confide in anyone in my community, I wrote a rambling letter to my parents, using them as confidants for the struggle between my conscience and my longing. Desperate for guidance, I asked them for advice in early 1971, though they were thousands of miles away and overseas mail often took weeks to arrive.

> Dear Mom and Dad,
>
> ...I am a different person than the seventeen-year-old who joined MMS. My ability to love one person and the joy of being loved by a man who knows me so well is rocking my foundation. I don't know how to reconcile my loyalty and commitment to my community and my vocation with what Gerard offers as a man.
>
> Everything is uncertain for me now. If I come to a decision to leave the community here, then I will get a job in the country and continue to see Gerard on a freer basis so I can evaluate our relationship apart from the huge pressures I feel. But I don't know if I am ready to leave my beloved MMS; it is just this group of sisters here that makes me so unhappy. Perhaps I will just take a year's leave of absence and continue working here in Malawi. Oh, I don't know what to think. You have never told me what I should do when I faced decisions, but I feel so desperate for an objective view. Am I giving up too easily in the face of the difficulties here, or do you think I am better suited for marriage? Do you have any advice for me?

Confused young woman that I was, and with no other recourse that I could see, I turned to my faraway parents when I was unable to make a decision that only I could make.

It all became too much for me. In mid-March 1971 I wrote a short note to Gerard asking that we take a break for a while. I had just finished listening to a long, love-filled tape he had mailed me and tried to record a response back . . . but couldn't do it. I wrote in my journal that night:

> I'm so tired these days, so very tired. There's nothing left in me to give.

CHAPTER FORTY-FOUR

ESCAPE

Those stresses filled my mind like an irrepressible Hydra in the early weeks of 1971. I continued to feel like an outsider at Phalombe, which was too large and too insular a community. I wanted a closer engagement with village life, not a Dutch enclave; I wanted to meet Malawians on their turf, not on mine; I wanted to do preventive health work rather than treating people after they were sick. I wanted a resolution with Gerard.

And most of all, I wanted an undivided heart.

As if my life weren't upside down enough, another man showed up. Robert, a self-assured British agriculturalist who had visited Norma and me once in Tengani on a Lower Shire tour with some other ex-pats, arrived in Phalombe and sought me out in the OPD. I didn't know what to make of his appearance, so I invited him to join us for the approaching meal. While he sat amidst all the sisters for lunch, he kept his eyes on me, directed his conversation to me. *What was going on? We hardly knew each other.* I began to obsess. Was I sending out some subtle message to men, secreting a scent like an animal in heat? Something was occurring beyond my intent or understanding. I felt like bait, even though I wasn't fishing.

The tensions pushed me to my edge. I worried for my emotional and physical health. Malaria seemed minor compared to the state I was in. I decided that I needed to get away—work elsewhere in the country, to see if distance would help me find peace.

A regional meeting of MMS leaders from several of our African missions was held at Phalombe around the time of my breaking point, and since their agenda included staffing, I made a request for a transfer. I was aware of the Private Hospital Association of Malawi (PHAM), since our district superior worked for them, and raised the possibility of finding work with that organization. It had been established in the mid-sixties as an ecumenical consortium of all the Christian churches providing medical services in Malawi.

In the first week of March 1971 I followed up with my local superior to further explain my request, focusing on my desire to do preventive village health work, with no mention of any other issues. She arranged a meeting with PHAM two days later in Blantyre.

The first half of that appointment was with the district superior at her PHAM office. She had disagreed with the Pilot Project from the beginning and was well aware of the tensions it created within the Phalombe community. We had an edgy exchange that left me uncertain whether she would support my application.

The next meeting with PHAM's executive director was cordial and gave me some hope. Mr. Lesser welcomed my inquiry and said he could see me in the mobile health unit based in Muona in the Lower Shire, but the position was currently filled. I left feeling that nascent hope slip through my fingers. I didn't know of any other options.

A few days later on an afternoon break I went to my room to reflect on my waning prayer life. It evolved into questioning Providence—the hand of God—in our personal histories. God had gone missing for me in those turbulent days when I most needed a sense of His presence. I went to supper without reaching a conclusion.

While doing the dishes after the meal, Sister Rose, an American MMS physician who had been consulting to PHAM for a few days, found me.

"Aimee, can I speak with you, privately?" My hands still had soap suds on them as I followed her to a small room. "The nurse who has been heading PHAM's mobile health team in the Lower Shire suddenly has to leave for health reasons. Could you do it for the next year and a half?"

It felt so providential I almost wanted to laugh. I wrote that night in my journal: "Okay, God, I believe you are still around." The position was ideal in many ways. I would live with a Canadian nurse volunteer while she trained me, receive a salary of forty-four pounds a month, have a room provided at the Muona hospital, and use of a car. Most of all, I'd have work that involved both a clinical and administrative role. It was the solution I had been searching for.

My four Pilot Project friends heard my news at next day's coffee break with mixed emotions—glad for me but sad to have me leave Phalombe. Later, I talked with two of them, and they expressed their own unhappiness living in that community and their uncertainties of what they would do next. They envied me that I was finding another place to live in the country we all loved.

That conversation was followed by a meeting with Sister Rose and Nancy, a bright-eyed Canadian volunteer a few years younger than me. I sensed an immediate connection. I left that meeting with the confidence that my future was decided for the next year and a half. I was jubilant and began shaping my plans in my journal:

> These coming weeks will be full ones: packing and finishing up my work, saying good-byes. I'm leaving the community here—such a relief—and starting again in a new place with unknown demands. This assignment should provide me enough time alone to reach some clarity about the pull between Gerard and my vocation.

> I shall probably wait until the end of March to go to Muona so I can leave the OPD in good order for whoever will take it over. I am eager to get started in direct village health work, where I'll have both professional and personal independence. I am so excited.

The prospect of returning to the familiar Lower Shire warmed my spirit; it felt like going home. But that location also would bring me closer to Gerard in Nsanje. That was not my intent, not at all a reason for accepting the PHAM job. It was just coincidental. In truth, I would have preferred to have more miles between Gerard and me while I tested myself in the new work, though I suspected he would be quite pleased to hear I would be within a two-hour drive from his mission.

What I didn't suspect was that the missionary "bush telephone" would judge my decision as driven solely by my desire to be near Gerard.

CHAPTER FORTY-FIVE

CHAFF PEOPLE

Leaving Phalombe, I struggled through emotional good-byes to my Pilot Project friends and the Malawian hospital staff and nurses, but my farewell to the Dutch sisters lacked similar emotions. I drove off without saying good-bye to those at the main house. Many of them didn't even know I was leaving, or maybe they were glad I was going. It didn't matter. I was disappearing, as in the novitiate days when a candidate or novice was suddenly gone one morning. Later, I reflected on the possibility that the sisters might have felt hurt and rejected by my choice to leave them. I don't know.

*

Five of us crammed in the car headed south: a driver from Muona hospital; Suzanne, a nurse from Scotland; Uta, a Dutch lab technician; Nancy; and myself. As the Mulanje Mountains receded into the fuzzy horizon behind me, the descent down the Cholo escarpment began. The fingers of the familiar gripped my heart as I returned to a place that held such memories: its miserable roads and arid landscape, the shimmering Shire River, Tengani, the impoverished yet generous Asena people . . . and Gerard.

The mountainous road was still dreadful and our little vehicle so weighted down we could only go one mile an hour. Rocks kept scraping the fenders. At one point we had to get out of the car for it to maneuver a treacherous turn. Then the near-mirage of the Shire River came into view, its silver path slithering through the barren landscape. I was arriving home.

Soon the Muona mission—the church, bishop's residence, hospital, and sisters' quarters—were outlined by scattered lights in the night. They had the luxury of a generator running full-time. A band of kids—the orphans living at the hospital—came running to greet our exhausted carload.

The apartment I would share with Nancy was in a wing of the hospital. Settling in, we heard the crying of babies from the isolation ward and the little ones next door in pediatrics. Inside our little space the heat lingered, the mosquito squads cruised, and the faucets yielded only drips of cold water. *Home Sweet Home,* I thought. Nancy and I had a hasty cup of tea, then dove under our nets to escape the bugs and pursue longed-for sleep.

Rising the next morning before light for our medical foray into the bush, we discovered there was *no* water in the faucet—*Was I in Tengani village again?* We dressed—without being able to wash—and packed up the PHAM Land Rover. I met the rest of the mobile health team: Mary, a Malawian midwife, and Joseph, the driver, who also did the wound dressings.

We later added another Malawian nurse and a general assistant who helped with non-medical tasks like carrying heavy supplies and weighing the babies. Once Nancy returned home to Canada, it would be the four Malawians and I traveling to the same seven villages each week.

At 7:00 a.m. we set off south on my first expedition to two villages, the closest being a ninety-minute drive south. We took the ferry across the river before enduring a brutal ride through the dense bush, its thick branches, like hands, whacking and grabbing at our vehicle. The rutted path through the dense underbrush jostled our bodies and knocked about the supplies in the back.

When we reached the first village of Masanduko, only a few women were waiting. "This is most unusual," Nancy muttered. We soon discovered we had a *mlandu* (conflict) on our hands. The chiefs and elders from several villages had a complaint. They had built a thatched roof in one area to protect the patients and our team from the searing sun, but in exchange for their efforts, they expected their people would receive free services. PHAM, our sponsor, charged only pennies for the care given, but the leaders felt even that was too much.

For the *mlandu*, Nancy, Mary, and I went into the shed and sat on hastily scrounged chairs. Eight chiefs and elders were seated across the table from us, surrounded by a crowd of men. The throng was intimidating. One man acted as moderator and stated both sides of the case. We asked Mary to be our spokesperson to assure the best communications, and Nancy and I whispered down the table to coach her what to say.

The other side of the table wasn't responding to our justification for the penny fees. After a half-hour of back and forth, I was hot and frustrated. Without a clear intention on my part, I popped up from my seat, asked to speak, and in my best Chichewa explained that we needed the money to buy medical supplies, pay the staff, buy petrol to get there—all of which we had explained before.

My impetuous action must have surprised them—and then they surprised us by agreeing. "Oh, now we understand. You may continue using the shed and the people will have to pay." We all shook hands. How reasonable.

They smiled and nodded to us after that. Right after the *mlandu*, I treated one of the chiefs, who had a badly infected lip. The rest of the elders queued up for the clinic and received their medicines. The line of villagers grew as they saw we were in business, so we had a good clinic with many people receiving needed care.

But another long drive in the midday heat awaited us: Nsangwe village where, again, only a few patients waited under a tree. I began joking with some of the women and heard the once-familiar Asena sounds. It was sweet to be able to differentiate the two dialects of Chichewa and Chisena. It was a short clinic. Nancy complained that this group was not responding to PHAM's focus on preventive health efforts, such as vaccines, anti-malarials, and infant nutrition, but came only when they were dreadfully sick.

On the ferry ride back to Muona, the Mulanje Mountains were clearly visible in the distance, but I felt no regrets that I wasn't there. Gone was the sense I had for so many months of being unrooted in the world. My roots were growing down into the Lower Shire's parched soil. I was right where I belonged.

After the long, sweaty ride home—the heat so intense I could grab hold of it—I relished the refreshing cold shower, thanks to the water flowing again. Working in temperatures of 100 to 120 degrees made me feel as if my blood were draining from my body, siphoning away my energy. I came to appreciate how hard it was to be industrious in the tropics. Layering on malaria and all the other endemic diseases the people carried in their bodies, it was amazing they could function at all.

Several of the village clinics we conducted had no table or surface for our supplies other than the ground, so everything got very dusty or muddy if it rained. A few places had no cover or protection from the sun. We set up under a tree with cloths laid out to hold our supplies. Sometimes I sat on the ground when I became weary from standing. It couldn't have been much more rudimentary. Once home we still had to clean and sterilize our needles, package the pills, sort out the bandages, and restock the Land Rover for the next round.

At the end of my first trip to two villages I was introduced to the mostly Belgian sisters who managed the hospital, and Nancy and I were invited to supper with the bishop. I was uncertain what to expect, not knowing what he might have heard of Gerard's frequent visits to Tengani and the house he allowed Norma, Yoli, and I to use for those three months. The conversation stayed light, except for one pointed comment he made about losing his priests. One had recently left to marry a British volunteer nurse he had met at Muona. The bishop's comment seemed pointed at me.

Afterwards, Nancy and I came back to our apartment and served as supper for the mosquitos who lived with us.

*

On Tuesday we ventured to Bangula, a Catholic mission where we had an indoor room in which to conduct the clinic. A huge crowd had already gathered as we pulled up. I listened to a class on healthy foods that Mary was teaching and then began seeing patients. While Nancy treated the babies a long line of adult patients awaited me, several of whom suffered from terrible leg ulcers and machete wounds. Because those knives were used for many daily activities, as well as weapons, people were always being injured by them, accidentally or on purpose.

New to the routine, my efforts to treat patients were uncoordinated; I kept bumping into Joseph, the wound dresser, as we both medicated and bandaged dozens of damaged limbs. We had to fight off the flies and get the ointments and wrappings on before they further infected the wounds.

The following day's clinic was based at the Makanga agriculture station, a program run by expatriates to teach modern agricultural methods. Nancy said it was always a short morning, so we planned on spending several hours reorganizing our supplies once home. She taught me how to place restock orders from the PHAM headquarters in Blantyre.

Ledza clinic on Thursday was the opposite of Makanga. Nancy said more ill people showed up than she had ever seen there. The lines of sick seemed endless. I was delighted, however, to meet a student I had taught at Likulezi, and we had a lovely reunion when the clinic was finally over. Back home at Muona my intended free afternoon never materialized because Nancy was fussing about the mobile health team's finances, and I helped her wade through the paperwork.

Dolo clinic was all mine the next day; it was a practice run for me without Nancy. I felt my history-taking was good, blending rudimentary Chisena and Chichewa and asking for help from the other staff when a case was out of the ordinary.

At Dolo I did my first incision of a dreadful, ready-to-burst boil on a man's leg, and was confronted by a woman with a swollen face caused by a grossly infected tooth. With no dentists in the Lower Shire, I had no option but try to pull the tooth to drain the infection. This was *way* out of my comfort zone—but that was true for everything I was doing. With Joseph's assistance, I did it. I only had a generic surgical forceps, and my hands were shaking badly. With no way to numb her jaw, I feared causing her pain, but fortunately for both of us, the badly decayed tooth came out without too much pulling.

When I got back to Muona from the hour-long ride home, I was in a celebratory mood after doing so well with what I called my first "Solo Dolo." Nancy had made a special chicken dish for our supper as a celebration.

Then came the weekend. Saturdays and Sundays were free for us, unlike in Phalombe, where I worked six days a week. Nancy and I usually joined the other volunteers for meals, or used the mission pool, wrote letters, did laundry, and ran errands. I didn't really think about it then, but I socialized with the lay volunteers rather than with the Muona sisters, who were European and still wearing habits. I felt more at home among the younger women than the older nuns. That was a strike against me in the eyes of the other missionaries.

The weekly cycle of clinics was fairly regular, with two held on alternating weeks. We were up at 5:30 a.m. and on the road by 7:00 a.m. before the sun began to burn up the land. The time of our return was always uncertain: the distances were long, the routes affected by the weather, and the number of patients unknown—from twenty to hundreds.

Nancy treated the babies, the midwife examined the pregnant mothers, and I cared for the adults. I treated a dreadful assortment of conditions: besides the ubiquitous malaria and hookworm, there were the severe anemias, bilharzia, elephantiasis, sleeping sickness, tuberculosis, pneumonia, snake bites, rabid dog bites, and the horrid tropical ulcers that developed from an infected cut or scratch and could become a gaping hole down to the bone. My nursing degree from Catholic University never prepared me for that spectrum of diseases.

My exposure to numerous villages brought a profound insight into their residents' lives. The Lower Shire Malawians were the chaff of the country, the poorest in the second-poorest nation of the world. They lived so intimately bound to their environment it seemed as if their bodies were pulled from the ground on which they laid each night, and arose wearing the dust and clay of the land. With no easy access to bathing, no hygiene products, no latrines anywhere, they and the earth were extensions of each other.

How could I allow myself to think about my personal turmoil when each day, at one village or another, a long queue of dispirited mothers held out their lethargic babies to us, their eyes beseeching us to make them better. When ancient, pencil-thin men and women swathed in rags walked long distances on cracked and oozing feet to have them bandaged? When children with worm-filled bellies shyly hid behind their mothers' legs, yet urgently needed attention?

How, indeed, could I think of myself? The immediacy of their needs, the shards of hope I could offer, and the short-term salve of medicines I prescribed consumed my attention until I was back in the Land Rover bumping toward home.

Then, though weary and perspiration-soaked, thoughts of my own dilemma crowded back into my consciousness, petty as they seemed in the face of what the people of the Lower Shire endured.

CHAPTER FORTY-SIX

DIMMED VISION

The first week of familiarizing myself with the mobile health unit challenged me: finding my way around the Muona compound where the team was based, stocking the Land Rover, interacting with the staff, learning the characteristics of each village population and location, and treating the diverse medical conditions each day. To me, taking preventive and intermediate medical care and compassion to the villages where the people lived made more sense than treating them in the strange environs of a Western hospital. Tengani had taught me so much. Within days of arriving in Muona and traveling with the mobile team, I knew I had found my niche. This was the type of public health work I wanted to do—and hoped to do well beyond my August 1972 contract. In spite of its inherent hardships, serving the poorest of the poor was the *reality* I had been searching for, the life I felt called to.

At the end of the work days, shared meals and evening get-togethers with local volunteers introduced me to a wide range of expatriates from numerous countries: England, Scotland, the Netherlands, and Germany. Some were young, single volunteers committing one or two years of service through various religious and governmental organizations, while others were more mature missionary couples from their home churches who had been in Malawi for years. Most of the younger volunteers in my age range worked at the Muona hospital: a doctor, a lab technician, two nurses. The instant connection and kinship among the group of us foreigners was refreshing after the lack of easy acceptance in Phalombe. I was the only nun living outside my religious community, the only American . . . but that all mattered less and less.

While new faces were entering my life, others were leaving. A harsh judgment ran through the missionary's bush telephone of a priest and nun who had run off to Rhodesia. My mail carried accounts of more sisters returning home: two of my MMS friends from our South African hospital, another from Dacca, East Pakistan. Gerard mentioned in his letters that, like him, several of our Likulezi priest classmates were disillusioned with the patronizing attitudes of their fellow missionaries and struggled with the gap between their missiology and that of the older, pre-Vatican II priests, long in Malawi. Word that Norma had been assigned to Swaziland struck hardest and burrowed a hole in me that held a deepening pool of sadness.

But my own vision was dimming as well. The Catholic faith that had brought me to Malawi seemed to be dissolving in the face of contradictory experiences.

At a Good Friday service in Muona church in 1971 I found that the rituals that had been so richly meaningful in the past now felt empty and irrelevant in the African environment. It was "the medium, not the message" that was the problem, as Marshall McLuhan wrote in 1964. I was also reading *Future Shock* at the time and saw its central theme embodied in the contrast between the Church in Malawi and in the States. I left before the service finished and returned to the apartment, craving sleep but only able to wrestle with my pillow.

Catholicism had been the air I breathed since childhood. My lungs inhaled the sacred; I longed for the Holy Other. Yet in Malawi, the prevailing church doctrines and missionary practices became untenable, irreconcilable with what was real around and in me.

Increasingly I began to hold at arm's length Catholic beliefs and rituals and to critically examine what previously I could not disentangle from my own identity.

The growing chasm became especially evident a day later, when I shared a potluck dinner and meaningful conversations with several other volunteer friends before we left for the Easter Vigil at the Muona church. We lined up in the back pew; the hospital nuns filled the front rows on both sides. Halfway through the sweltering and lengthy service, the group of us signaled each other and we left to go for a swim, returning in time for Communion.

My friends and I walked the length of the church aisle to receive the host from the bishop. Those sisters in the pews could observe my still-wet hair and my *nsaru* skirt wrapped around me. This would not have been an issue for the lay volunteers, but what silent judgments must have run through the minds of the bishop and sisters about me—a nun.

For someone normally sensitive to the feelings and opinions of others, I had become oblivious to the impact of my behavior on the religious community around me, to how my actions estranged me from them. It was not intentional, nor an act of belligerent flaunting; rather, my compass was off kilter. The boundaries for appropriate nun behavior, once so clear to me, were lost. The pressures of the past year had split my psyche into separate selves that I couldn't hold together; I no longer knew who I was.

Those stress cracks were compounded by the letters and telegrams arriving from home in early 1971 about my father's failing health. In March, as I prepared to commit to PHAM for a year and a half, my mother wrote that my father had suffered a series of heart attacks, then was diagnosed with tuberculosis, followed by the prospect of brain surgery for an aneurism. My dear mother's communications carried the weighty worry of the unknown. Telegrams arrived days after they were sent, throwing me into constant uncertainty about my father's condition. I sent one telegram and longer letters offering to come home if they needed me. I was still their oldest, dutiful daughter. Then I'd wait a week or two for updated news from my mother. In late March 1971 I hung on a twisting cord, suspended between preparing to go home and my contract with PHAM.

My heart couldn't have been more divided.

CHAPTER FORTY-SEVEN

THE VISE

On April 6, 1971, early in my second week of traveling to the various villages with PHAM's mobile team, I was in the midst of dispensing medicines at Bangula clinic when I turned to see Gerard coming into the room. My heart flipped; my whole body flushed. I hadn't seen him for a month. He left quickly after jerking his head in the direction of the door he had come through. Once I finished with the last few patients, I joined him outside for a brief walk. Gerard was visibly upset. "The bishop and Father Richard know about us. We need to talk. Can we meet later . . . this afternoon?" Then he quickly left.

I was anxious about the significance of his news but excited to see him. Weeks later, Nancy described to Gerard how I had bustled around the apartment, humming while I changed my clothes and spritzed my body with rose water to counter the smell of sweat. Once he arrived, the three of us chatted for a short time until Nancy discreetly left.

After a brief embrace, I could read in Gerard's body the deep stress he was enduring, so I held back and listened as he gave a few more details. We huddled together like hostages to decide what to do with this new information. Clearly, our relationship was known in the Lower Shire missionary community, though we shouldn't have been surprised. Every piece of news became village gossip and was quickly on everyone's lips. It was like having a Big Brother with unclosing eyes, flapping ears, and a loose tongue. We decided that Gerard should speak to the bishop about our relationship and ask his guidance; he would come back if the bishop would meet with us together.

A vise was beginning to tighten around us.

After Gerard departed, his bent shoulders carrying the weight of his mission, I confessed my relationship to Nancy. Her ready understanding relieved me. As a non-Catholic she didn't have the church's judgment of us and was able to appreciate the naturalness of our attraction. She confided that she had been involved with Geoffrey, the young doctor at Muona Hospital. It was a balm to share our emotional lives, woman to woman, and a decision clarified as I poured out a bewildering mix of feelings to her.

I felt I should leave Medical Mission Sisters but wanted to stay with PHAM's mobile health team for as long as I could. Once the district superior returned in a few days I would ask for a meeting to discuss my commitments.

The next day, April 7, I received a letter Gerard sent back with Suzanne, one of my volunteer friends who had been in Nsanje shopping.

My dear Aimee,

When I met with the bishop yesterday I was calm, felt I was talking about the most natural matter in the world. It was a good meeting. The bishop understands much better than I expected. He had heard about our relationship from others. He mentioned that Father Richard also knew and felt that one of us had to go. The bishop's main concern is the fear of my departure. He said, "I hope you'll not be leaving me. I have no one else to cover Nsanje until Father Paul returns from his sabbatical in October." He was relieved when I said that I would stay until that time, at least.

Regarding our relationship the bishop said, "Please be discreet while you are working this out." He was not bitter but open and frank. I explained that we understood the problems of us both remaining here but that you wanted to continue your PHAM work. He is willing to meet with you alone, but not together.

So I am pleased that he understands and we can continue to search for the best decision in the coming weeks.

Feel free and happy with me, Aimee.

Yours, Gerard

All seemed calm over the next few days. I carried on with the village clinics and didn't see Gerard again until he and Pieter arrived in Muona for a meeting six days later. The two stopped at my apartment to invite me to Norma's upcoming farewell party at Njale. Gerard and I had no chance for a tête-à-tête with Pieter there.

Later that afternoon I went to Father Richard's office in Bangula to ask if I might ride with him to the party. I used the visit to discreetly beg some time to discuss my relationship with Gerard. Father didn't respond or show any facial reaction, shuffling papers on his desk while I stood there, waiting. It was as though he hadn't heard me—or didn't want to. I crept out the door, spurned.

My growing sense of urgency, coupled with the bishop's apparent willingness to talk with me, propelled me to seek a meeting with him. Trusting in an exchange similar to Gerard's I walked in, trembling but hopeful.

An angry, towering six-foot man of God in white stood up when I entered his office, stared down on my small frame, and began shouting at me: "I won't allow it! I won't allow it! Why did you ever come here? I will not lose any more of my priests!"

Those vitriolic words from his quivering mouth fell on my body like hot embers, singeing my soul. Embedded in his anger was the patriarchal belief that a woman is the temptress—that I had seduced Gerard.

Stunned, unable to find my voice, I bowed my head before him—breaking a long ago promise to myself that I would never do that. The bishop abruptly dismissed me from his chambers into the searing African sun, a scarlet letter slapped onto the back of my sweaty blouse.

I stumbled back to my apartment. Betrayed. Shamed. Frightened. Alone. I was at a breaking point and cried and thought in circles for hours. Nancy finally arrived home to find me in a heap. She was shocked and couldn't believe my story.

Alone later that evening and needing to try to regain some sense of personal control, I wrote my classmates at Njale that I wouldn't be coming to Norma's party. I also wrote the superior at Phalombe to ask for a meeting. I knew she would probably hear from the bishop or the district superior, who knew each other well. Then I poured myself into a pathetic letter to my parents, unable to speak of anything other than my own turmoil, despite Dad's serious medical problems.

Dear Mom and Dad,

It's been a rough week. After Gerard spoke to the bishop about our situation, I met with the bishop. Went badly. There is pressure for either Gerard or me to leave, and Gerard promised the bishop to stay at Nsanje until October.

Since Dad seems to be stable, I'll stay with the mobile health unit unless you need me to come home. I wrote PHAM's director that I may need to leave by the end of the year so he has time to find a replacement, which won't be easy. I need to inform the bishop and Gerard. I'd really like to finish my contract, which runs until August of '72—or even stay longer, but it is so tense here on the Muona compound with the bishop and sisters. I imagine they all look down on me. I wish I was tougher and wouldn't let their opinions bother me— but I'm not.

I'll be all right though. Don't worry.

At the end of Bangula clinic on the day of Norma's party, I told Father Richard I wasn't going to the gathering. I hoped he might ask why and open a conversation . . . but he didn't and I couldn't.

That evening loneliness circulated through me as I thought of all my classmates together in Njale without me. Gerard was there, unaware of my terrible treatment by the bishop. I also was grieving that I wasn't able to say good-bye to Norma. She had told me that she wasn't sure if she was going to return to Malawi after her four months in Swaziland. And I felt sorry for myself, cut off from everyone.

Fortunately Norma and Flora drove down to Makanga clinic the following day and found me as I was finishing up. What a joy and relief to have friends to talk with, if only for a few hours.

Arriving back at my apartment, we met Gerard, who was in Muona in hopes of seeing me. After he heard about the bishop's accusatory and humiliating treatment, Gerard was furious at him and pained for me. He had to return to Nsanje shortly. I told him I would not meet with the bishop again without him.

On April 15 I returned from Ledza clinic exhausted, having treated 175 patients alone, and found Gerard at my apartment, wanting to further mull over our options. Since he had promised the bishop to stay, I was on the chopping block. Hoping to call upon the bishop's compassion, I told Gerard I'd write the bishop and explain that neither of us had intended this to happen; we both loved our work and were trying to find an honest way through the complicated situation. We just needed a little time to decide what was the best thing to do. I would also mention that I sympathized with how difficult it was for the receiving missionary community to understand and incorporate us newcomers.

When Gerard mentioned to the bishop later that day that I was going to write him, he retorted, "Is she afraid I won't understand otherwise?" Upset by his tone, Gerard said, "No, but when she met with you she wasn't able to speak and now wants to try to clearly explain herself."

It took only one day after my letter to the bishop for a sarcastic note to arrive at my apartment. The main message was that I was a disgrace to my community of sisters. It finished with, "What help would you expect from anyone who has lived so long in the missionary 'subculture' as you call it? The gap is not real—it's just created by you."

CHAPTER FORTY-EIGHT

DENOUEMENT

On April 22 I received a telegram that my father needed brain surgery. On April 23 Nancy and I traveled to Blantyre to take care of PHAM business and get our car repaired. I stopped in at the sole travel agency to check flights for the US in case I would have to leave on short notice if Dad's condition became critical. The delayed messages from home threw me back and forth against a wall of worry. The ride to town was filled with conflicted thoughts of returning home. In Blantyre, one of the Phalombe sisters shopping in town picked me up for the drive to Phalombe. I had no expectations of a warm welcome from my community there, and I was not disappointed.

The next day I sought out the local superior. We walked and talked for almost an hour. I gave her a broad outline of recent events from my viewpoint, though I didn't tell her of my thoughts of leaving MMS. I'm not sure why. I had felt so much criticism during my months there that I was hesitant to open myself more to her.

At the end of our walk, she advised me: "Leave the country for your own sake." *What did that mean—for my sake?*

That evening, unable to think clearly, I went through my meager possessions to see what I might pack for home—if and when the time came.

As no one could drive me back to Blantyre on April 25, I raced to catch a bus into town. It was a long, five-hour ride, with stops every fifteen minutes. Baskets, bundles, bodies, and chickens filled the crowded, noisy, smelly vehicle. Two men drunk on *mowa* in the seats in front of me argued over paying for bananas they'd bought along the route. I shrank back into my bench to avoid getting caught in the middle. I was grateful to reach Blantyre intact.

A mutual friend had notified Gerard of my probable arrival in Blantyre in the late afternoon. Filthy and fatigued from the bus ride, I cleaned up in the women's washroom at the Shire Hotel, a vestige of colonial days. Gerard was in the lounge, anxiously awaiting my arrival. In one of its dark corners, we drank cold Fanta sodas and I whispered to him in panicked tones about the recent conversation in Phalombe. "What did she mean—leave for my own sake? What would happen if I don't? Do we have *any* control over our future?"

Needing to meet Nancy soon, I walked with Gerard to his car. Once inside it, a sense of impending tragedy tinged our kisses before he drove me to Mt. Soche Hotel, where I was to meet Nancy for the drive back down the Cholo escarpment to Muona. When Gerard and I hugged good-bye, he was trembling. We were two drowning bodies being pulled from each other by strong currents.

Back in Muona and after Nsangwe clinic the next day, I wrote to the district superior informing her that I wanted to leave MMS but work for another six months to give PHAM time to find a replacement, assuming my father's condition wouldn't require that I return home quickly.

On Wednesday, April 28, I did Mkanga clinic without Nancy, as she had to go up to Blantyre on business. I was looking forward to the next few days alone. In the late hours, Uta, the lab tech, came and asked me to give my O+ blood for a woman cut up with a machete by an angry husband. Uta had to dig into my veins four times for one pint of blood. Somehow having to endure the pain of her repeated skin punctures with those ragged needles mirrored my own emotional pain.

The following day I managed the Ledza clinic—long lines of suffering people I had to treat alone. Once home, I found a letter in the post box from the district superior on PHAM letterhead. I stood there on the spot and read: "You are terminated immediately out of concern for missionary interests."

Shaking, I found my way to my empty apartment and fell into a maelstrom, barely afloat in swirling waters the rest of the night. Her words burned in my mind, over and over—*"You are terminated."*—*"You are terminated."* My soul was roiling with disparate emotions: guilt, relief at the thought of escaping all this turmoil, dread of leaving Gerard and Malawi, a sense of shame I couldn't shake. *Why wasn't Nancy here when I needed her?* I would have driven to Gerard hours away in Nsanje, but Nancy had the car.

I couldn't leave immediately as told—there was the next day's clinic to do; the people were expecting us. As I set out for Dolo village in the morning, the Land Rover—mirroring my own state—jerked to a halt with a sudden flat tire, requiring a lengthy repair on the spot. Once we finally reached Dolo, I dragged through clinic, fighting lack of sleep and numbness over my termination.

Back home after the day's work, I prayed for a letter from my folks with an update on Dad, thinking it might be my way out. There was nothing in the post box. I spent the afternoon in an exhausted sleep. When I woke, I began to think about having to pack my few things. I had been working on the mobile health team for only two months.

In those desolate days, I felt forsaken by God and man.

CHAPTER FORTY-NINE

BROKEN

The next few days were soggy with grief; I barely recall them. A hurricane had ripped through my life, pulling up all the tree roots and tossing houses in tangled piles. I was in shock.

After the district superior's dismissal letter, I packed my few things over the weekend while waiting for Nancy to return so she could prepare to take over the clinics.

I felt like a young woman forced to have an abortion, denied a say in a decision that changed the rest of my life—a wooden marionette, controlled by others.

That Monday, Nancy returned from Blantyre with mail. In the small pile was a letter for me, which simply said that I was to return immediately to Phalombe—or else. I didn't know what the *or else* could be.

Then, shaking her head in disbelief, Nancy went on to report that she had run into Geoffrey, just back in Muona from Blantyre. He asked her, "What's Aimee been up to? Rumors are flying in town that she is going to be deported by President Kamuzu Banda for something she 'did' with Father Prinsen."

When Nancy told me this, I crumpled onto the nearby chair. *What kind of a nightmare was I in? Why was everyone trying to accuse me? And of what?* It was ridiculous to think that scholarly Father Prinsen, our teacher, had anything to do with me. I hadn't seen him in months—and the President of Malawi? *It was insanity!*

I felt caught in an African version of a Salem witch hunt.

That rumor was the final assault. I was beaten, saw no way to fight or resist what was happening. No way to defend myself. *To whom would I go for help?* I didn't know what to do, where to turn. I was being led to the guillotine and couldn't escape my fate. My years of obedience denied me any sense of autonomy, any possibility to even consider saying, "No, I won't go. I'm staying here." But realistically, without the PHAM job, I had no income, no place to live, no means of transport, no ground to stand upon.

And a judging voice inside said I had brought it on myself.

I dashed off a quick note to Gerard for Nancy to deliver to him in Nsanje and arranged rides to Blantyre and Phalombe.

*

Padrick Depta, a Malawian hospital staff who was going to town from Muona, brought me to Blantyre. When he was dropping me off, he asked in a gentle voice, "When are you coming back, Sister Aimee?" He had such a kind look in his eyes, I started crying.

While I was being driven to Blantyre, farewells unsaid, Gerard was sitting in his bedroom writing this letter to me:

> *Aimee, What a black day! I was shocked to hear that you have to leave soon. I drove frantically to Muona this morning and met both Christine and Nancy, who were so sad. Nancy said you meant so much to her and she had learned so much from you in the past weeks. She told me of the rumors of deportation. Aimee, I feel so responsible for you, so hopeless, so far away. Why did you leave so suddenly? Write me what you find out about the real reason of your dismissal. I'm thinking it is connected with me and then I have no other choice than to leave. I feel so responsible for the whole evolution. Why the hell must you be the one who has to go? God help us. Don't give up. Keep your pride—there are not many people like you here in Malawi. I hope to see you soon, once you write me of what's happening. Tell me how we can meet.*

I had been told to call the district superior when I reached Blantyre. No words were exchanged about why I was being dismissed. Once she confirmed that I had left Muona and was on my way to Phalombe, she abruptly ended the call, leaving me with half words caught in my throat.

One of the Phalombe sisters picked me up at midday in town near the Kandodo grocery store. We did the needed shopping she had come for, which took time. Because many of the local Indians left when their stores were closed by President Banda, supplies were less available and had to be hunted down. Her task finished as best she could, we went on to Phalombe. Most of the sisters didn't expect me.

That evening, the superior and senior doctor came to my room and informed me I was being sent home because of my relationship with Gerard. Nothing else appeared to matter: not the valuable work I was doing on the mobile health team, not my unfinished contract with PHAM that was leaving the organization without a nurse, not the fact that I loved my work and the Malawian people, and they me—none of it held any weight against my sin. I tried to explain my side of the story, talked about the added stress that repeated letters about my father's serious illness had on me, complicating timely decisions between Gerard and me. In the end, however, the decision to send me home had been made.

I returned to town on May 5 to make my plane reservations. *How could I endure such opposing emotions: wanting to stay, wanting to escape?* I arranged to see friends in Frankfurt, Amsterdam, and, hopefully, Clare in London, as I worked my way toward the States. I hoped it would be a comfort to talk with her. My mood swung from a sense of freedom and expectancy to fear and grief. It was all upside down and backward. *How did I get to that precipice?*

*

The few days I had in Phalombe before leaving Malawi were spent saying good-bye to my many Malawian friends, the hospital and compound staff, as well as the sisters who were apparently told—I don't know what—about my departure. How they felt about it I would never know. They were such tight-lipped women when it came to expressing feelings.

I felt like a pariah.

I did have a long conversation with Fiona, a lay-nurse living with the community. She was the only one who reached out to me and expressed support. She said she was sure that I would marry Gerard.

I spent many hours writing letters to the people I hoped to visit on my return layovers and to my family in Philadelphia. I didn't write to the American motherhouse, assuming they would be told. I couldn't bear to be the one to let them know I had failed them.

I also spent time raising the hems on my few dresses and skirts. President Kamuzu Banda disapproved of the shorter skirts popular then. In Malawian culture, showing a woman's legs was like showing a woman's breast in the US. Every woman had to wear her skirt well below her knees. If found in a short skirt in public, a Malawian policeman would likely cut her hems with his knife right there on the street—or she could be sent to jail. This had produced an ugly new style. Foreign women had added layers of ruffles or additional fabric to lengthen their clothes if there wasn't enough hem to let out. I was sewing up the hems so I didn't return home looking like someone out of the 1940s. The sewing gave me something to focus my mind on when I felt at risk of losing it.

I received two distraught letters from Gerard. He was so upset he didn't know what to do with himself and asked me what he should do. Why was I being sent away? Should he come to Phalombe—or would that create more problems for me? Should he also leave in protest? He was hanging on tenterhooks and didn't realize how few remaining days I had. He talked as though we had weeks to still meet and talk. When I conveyed through friends that I was leaving soon and the first and last time I would see him was that Sunday on the way to the airport, he was broken by grief. What a cruel meeting that would be.

I could hardly bear all the weights on my back, but in the midst of those painful last days, two surreal incidents occurred.

Handsome British Robert sent a message to me, asking me to dinner. *Dinner? In Phalombe? How did he know I was leaving?* The bush telephone was so efficient. I found his invitation disconcerting, but said he could come to say good-bye, unclear why he felt the need to do so. When he arrived, with no thought about what any of the sisters were thinking when he showed up, I asked him to drive me to Likulezi so I could say good-bye to Father Prinsen and the catechists, and we could chat on the way. On the short drive back, he confessed his love and asked me to marry him and return to Kenya, where he had a cattle ranch. I stared at him in disbelief.

Why would he ask a near stranger to marry? We had only met and talked on two or three occasions. Why me? I said no, pleading my uncertainties about everything. When he let me out of his car, he handed me a letter and told me not to read it until I was on the plane.

*

It was almost a year since I had seen Father De Groot in Muloza, and just days before I was to leave, he came to Phalombe and sought me out. He found me sitting alone in the hospital courtyard. When I saw him, shame welled up in me. I dreaded losing his respect. Tears seeped out as I began to tell him that I was leaving, but he already had heard through the missionary grapevine. It was why he came. His face was crinkled with sadness, and he seemed not to be able to talk but only shake his head, saying, "Aimee, Aimee." I didn't sense he was judging me but sharing my sorrow over the loss of my dream, shared with him as we sat by his living room fire.

As he started to walk away, he turned, gazed into my tear-filled eyes, and whispered his final words: "I'll never forget those two weeks. They were one of the happiest times in my life."

Those two incidents confused me but also made me feel valued. I needed to feel there were people who cared about me as my days in Malawi were running out.

It was raining that day. I wondered if the raindrops were tears—mine or those of others who were sad to see me go.

Sunday May 9, 1971, was D-Day. I was nauseated and couldn't swallow anything. All the sisters came to say their good-byes when the car pulled up to the main living quarters. Not many words were spoken, so I don't know what they felt: pity? Embarrassment at my actions as one of them? Relief that I was going? I teared up as I said the last good-bye, but then I was in the car and took my last look at Phalombe compound fading away in the dust from the car's tires.

Accompanied by Pat, Flora, and Yoli, my Pilot Project friends who would remain in Malawi—two of them for only a short time—we made the tension-filled drive from Phalombe to Blantyre, where we met Gerard at a rendezvous point. Gerard's face was haggard, his shoulders drooping in helplessness. He and I had some quiet time together in a small park. Gerard swore his unending love for me; promised that he would leave by October, and then we would be together in either America or the Netherlands. Deep in shock and grief, I could only whisper, "I hope so."

The group of us then drove to the Shire Hotel, where several of our priest classmates met us for something to eat—another "last supper," though I still couldn't eat anything. Pat wrote later of that time: "I remember all of us squeezed into a booth together, as if the pressure of feeling ourselves so close would prevent this from happening. It seemed too impossible. Looking back, I was in a state of shock after learning you were   being sent home."

By the time we all reached the airport, I was on autopilot, unable to do more than stick a tight smile on my face. I drank my last Fanta, shared the crazy jokes that reflected our year and a half together, then heard, "Flight #16 to Nairobi, now board-ing." The moment of separation had come.

Leaden legs resisted each step that took me away from Gerard and my friends, huddled at the edge of the airport gate. I felt like a shackled prisoner led to the gallows. My eyes were brewing more tears than I could cry in a day, in a week . . . for the rest of my life.

Loss, disgrace, and defeat were weeping wounds in my spirit. I was being sent home from Malawi and its people, exiled from a life I had waited ten years to experience, separated from a man I loved.

I tried to appear calm as I broke away, flashed Gerard the three-fingered sign language for *I love you* that we all used, but it was a pathetic last gesture.

Moving away from my dear companions and the crucible time we had shared, a foolish glance back showed Gerard, his head bent over to hide his tears. *Would I ever see him again?* I crossed my Rubicon as I walked to the waiting plane.

Onboard, I was grateful to be seated on the far side where I couldn't see the people left behind. Once in flight, I started my last journal entry to capture that defining moment of leaving:

> I've just left Malawi. It's 5:45 p.m. I was tearless as I hugged each friend, gave a brief kiss to Gerard, walked to the plane.
>
> My tears came at the moment of lift off, that eternal moment of suspension when one separates from the earth—a particular place with its particular people.
>
> Malawi is in twilight, but now above the clouds, I see the last rays of the setting sun. The engine's droning is the background music for the endlessly repeating thoughts: You are leaving Malawi, leaving Gerard, Pat,

Flora, and Yoli, Phalombe, the Lower Shire, the kind
and gentle Malawians—leaving—leaving—leaving.

My thoughts were interrupted when my elderly seat companion turned to me and asked, "So, tell me, young lady of the tears—why are you leaving Malawi?"

CHAPTER FIFTY

EMPTYING MY LIFE

Malawi was a crucible. In those broken years following my exile, I was a cracked vessel—no longer able to hold the holy water of commitment to anything—or anyone. It took years to patch together an identity from the fragments of my beliefs, aspirations, and self-trust shattered in those seventeen months. I didn't know the term then, but I was suffering from what in recent years has been called Post Traumatic Stress Disorder (PTSD).

The huge inequities between my life and that of the Malawians was a persistent taunt to my conscience. My prized vow of poverty had become a farce when confronted by the unrelenting deprivations of the Malawians. My vow of chastity left me with a scarlet letter on my back. My vow of obedience had betrayed me. Looking back on my months in Malawi, I came to the grim realization that conflict had been woven through the fabric of my days there: with the missionary community, with colonialism and patriarchy, with my sisters, my commitments, my dreams—with myself.

My flight from Malawi in 1971 took me through Nairobi, Frankfurt, Amsterdam, London, New York, and finally to my family home in Havertown, Pennsylvania—the home I thought I'd never enter again when I left that October day in 1960 to join Medical Mission Sisters.

It was a balm to be back within its walls, within the arms of my family, who loved me regardless of the reason behind my sudden return. I had kept my parents informed of all the issues though my letters and tapes. They were simply thrilled to have their oldest daughter back from Africa, no questions asked—and I rarely spoke of my feelings to them, or anyone.

My parents had recently sold the house, needing to scale down for the sake of Dad's health. In a month, 1205 Larchmont Avenue would no longer belong to them—or to me. I helped my family through the moving process, bereft that I had no sooner returned to the mother space of my childhood, often in my dreams, when it was taken from me.

Years of travel and many residences have never replaced our Havertown home as my heart's cradle.

*

I had spent a few days at the MMS motherhouse after my return from Malawi, but my sense of shame and failure had me skirting the edges of community gatherings and avoiding interactions with those in authority. I feared I was a *persona non grata*. I couldn't bear the potential judgment on the faces of those who might know why I was back.

In the summer of 1971, rather than living at the motherhouse, I asked to stay at my parents' bungalow in New Jersey to help them through the move and Dad's recuperation. Sisters were now able to spend needed time with their families, a normalcy not allowed in my early years in the community.

A dense fog surrounded me those first months. The most ordinary activities required huge effort: getting dressed, brushing my teeth, eating, doing laundry, cleaning—it all felt exhausting. An observer might have thought I was okay, but I was a robot trying to get through each day without collapsing.

I remember how, as a child swimming at the Jersey Shore, a huge wave would crash down on me, its surge tumbling then dumping me onto the beach. That was how I felt in those broken-shell months after Malawi—splattered.

*

One rainy New Jersey morning in August, three months after my return, I was alone at my parents' house when the heavy, black phone on the desk rang. My American superior was on the other end and went right to the point: "Aimee, do you plan to take a year's leave of absence or leave our community and seek dispensation from your final vows?"

I was stunned by her question. There had been no prior discussion. I had not even considered making that decision yet. It was still a challenge to choose what to eat for breakfast. I leaned against the wall for support. She waited, a silent void between us.

Thinking to give myself more time to consider what I wanted—needed—to do, my rational mind inched toward saying the words: "I will take a leave of absence." But before that sentence completed its path from my brain to my lips, an unknown voice shot up from my belly and announced into the phone: "I will leave." Her response was quick: "Very well. I will submit the request. You will receive the papers of secularization from Rome in a few weeks." Then she hung up.

My mind protested: "No wait, I didn't mean to leave! I don't know who said that!" But I just stood there, a pillar of salt, the handset pressed to my ear, wondering whose voice it was that had just decided my fate. That is how I remember it.

I unwittingly left my beloved Medical Mission Sisters that day.

*

More than two years after my flight home from Malawi, I found myself touring Europe—on $10 a day—with a friend in 1973. We had arrived in the Holy City of Rome. I was a different person from the one who visited there on her way to Africa. Then it was a kiss; now it was a slap.

In Rome I could have visited the Generalate and Mother Dengel, but I still carried a sense of failure about the Pilot Project, and shame lingered like a cloud around my head.

I didn't go to see her.

Instead, my friend and I assumed the role of young female tourists, and I focused on the city's beauty, nightlife, and scrumptious Italian food.

Midway through our stay, we were meandering along a second-story portico in the Vatican museum when, looking down into the courtyard below, I noticed a huge wooden gate at the far end swing open. A stream of black limousines tailed each other into the space and lined up along a walkway underneath me. Peering over on tiptoes to see what was occurring, I spied movement at another large door to the far right below. It opened and out flowed a queue of cardinals in their flamboyant purple and red regalia. One by one, each man doddered to his own private limo. A waiting chauffeur removed the cardinal's biretta from his head and then pivoted him so his eminence could sink into the rear seat.

Contemplating this dissonant scene, absorbing the piercing truth that it was those elderly, pampered men whose decisions determined the lives of millions of Catholics around the world and the impoverished African converts I had lived among, I felt the inside of my body shatter, as if it had been lined with glass. I heard the *cracking, tinkling, jingling* as the pieces fell inside me, down to my feet.

Without a protesting thought, I left the Catholic Church that day on the Vatican portico, a lifetime of beliefs abandoned.

*

The final loss was Gerard, for which I accept full responsibility. After I returned to the States I pulled down, not a veil, but a wall, between myself and Malawi . . . and him. I couldn't separate Gerard from the disastrous events that had changed the course of my life.

During that first year home, he continued to send long letters and soulful tapes from Nsanje, where he suffered profound loneliness in that isolated mission.

In early December 1971 Gerard returned to the Netherlands, intending to leave the priesthood. His letters to me continued: optimistic, persuasive, reminding me of the trust he had placed in me, in us. If I preferred, he was willing to come to the States to reunite and hopefully marry.

Back home I was thrust into a strange new singles life, which had been transformed by the freedoms of the seventies. The experience of being pursued by males confused me. I didn't know how to sort out attractions from love, so I dated other men and began to question my relationship with Gerard, wondered if it was the intensity of Africa that had fueled the relationship. I recognized how confused I felt about men's interest in me and began to doubt our love, my love.

The PTSD symptoms I had been experiencing were intensified in the middle of that dark time. In April 1972, my father suddenly died. A few months later my mother was diagnosed with cancer. I sat by her hospital bed while she cried, pleading for my father and complaining to God why her Tom wasn't there for her.

I could hardly bear it all.

Gerard's letters ended only when I wrote him in 1973 that I felt incapable of being the woman he wanted, unable to reciprocate his love. His confusion and desolation were palpable on the pages of his final letter.

> *There is no peace nor happiness in my heart. To be honest I feel really sad and nervous ... This week has been one of the worst in my life. I'm not angry at you—that wouldn't be fair ... I'm not knowing where to go. I don't feel interested in anything ... and I do know that this is a dangerous situation and I hope it will not last long. It is really against my character to be like this.*
>
> *It seems so incredible to me that we shall never meet again. I feel I have lost much. God bless you forever and thanks for all you gave me.*
>
> *Gerard*

I grieved for the heartbreak I caused him, only adding to the mountain of self-reproach I heaped on myself. And I grieved for myself, for not knowing how to be a free woman comfortable with blending sexuality with emotional and spiritual love, for not knowing what I wanted for my life. At thirty, I was still an adolescent in a woman's body.

Not having found myself yet, I gave up the man who would have been an excellent partner to live and work in Africa with me—a life I often fantasized about in later years.

*

As Malawi has receded into a shrouded period in my life over the past forty years, regret has been my silent companion, the ghost that hovers at my sight's periphery, the coattail that disappears around the corner. Regret is at the heart of this story. I regret that I left Malawi without a fight to stay there, that I wasn't mature enough to give my relationship with Gerard the chance it deserved, that I wasn't strong enough to be a faithful Medical Mission Sister.

On the eve of my departure for Africa, I had written in my journal:

> My hope for this life ahead is to rub noses with the truest elements of reality—but I fear that my expectations are too big to squeeze into my own five-and-ten-cent self... To be all that I want to be is one thing; to be all that I am able to be, quite another... Maybe my time in Africa will be the chance to forge the difference, discern that elusive reality I search for, when my tiny world encounters the larger one. Will I be still standing at the end?

Well, I wasn't still standing when I returned from my encounter with the larger world. I had been less than I could have been, less than I wanted to be. I had lived with an idealized image of myself. Though I had lived through an extraordinary time, I came home a five-and-ten-cent woman who still had to find her true worth.

In a letter mailed to me in 1972, a year after I left Malawi, John Patrishu, a student in my Likulezi first-aid class, wrote these touching words about the students' continued feelings toward me: "We do not know that our love will end."

He could not know how prescient his words would be for me, decades later.

Love and regret—birthed in Malawi like Siamese twins—are bound together so tightly, I cannot tease them apart . . . even today.

CONTINUED REVELATIONS

MR. MEHTA

Though their names may be changed, every person in this story is real—except for Mr. Mehta.

I began to draft the opening chapter based on my return flight from Malawi. I was unsure where the story would go until an elderly Indian gentleman showed up in the seat beside Sister Aimee and initiated a conversation. I didn't know who he was or why he appeared when he did. He wasn't a real person.

After his surprising arrival in my memoir, I researched the origins of Asians in Malawi. Most came from North India's Gujarat province in the 1800s to work on the railroads. They stayed and evolved into the merchant and business class. Further research on typical Gujarati family names revealed that one surname, Mehta, means "spirit or guide." I knew in that moment that Mehta was the name of my companion, the receptive listener to my story.

Perhaps if Mr. Mehta had been by my side during those months of turmoil in Malawi—a nonjudgmental advisor—I might not have been on that homebound plane in 1971.

THE SISTERS IN MALAWI

I realize now that the impression I gave of that community of sisters lacks balance. My journals and memory painted them with the same brush, but I see now that a critical few distorted my memories of the caring, gentle sisters who were kind to me.

Research at the MMS Philadelphia archives in 2012 on the development of the Cultural Orientation Project Experiment (COPE) revealed that the regional superior and sisters in Phalombe expressed serious concerns about placing the project in Malawi, but it was pressed on them, causing misplaced conflicts between the Dutch sisters and the five of us in that COPE Pilot Project. Deep, inherent tensions arose, which most of us weren't able to overcome.

During my time there I felt repeatedly judged and rejected by that group of sisters, but a 1971 letter from Gerard that I recently read has created confusion for me. In that letter he copied a note sent to him from my Phalombe superior on the very day I was leaving Malawi:

Dear Father Gerard,

I would have liked to help in a better way, but that was impossible because of pressure from outside. I would that Aimee and you had been given the chance to come to an honest decision. I knew already quite a long time about your relationship; there are always people who feel forced to inform me. I can only hope and pray that everything will be all right for both of you.

We all have tried to give Aimee a good and peaceful week in Phalombe before she leaves. We have shared good and difficult moments; we will miss her. She was very brave and I have got still more respect for her. I know it is clear you have very difficult times ahead. I hope you experience my sympathy for both of you. Strength for you, especially for today, May 9, when she leaves.

Cordial feelings,
Sister Irena

I was stunned when I read that note and don't know what to make of it. Why did she write him and not me? Did she feel she couldn't go against higher authorities by showing support for me? Perhaps I have forgotten something she might have said to me before I left Phalombe.

Or did I just stumble upon a truth that has eluded me until the moment of writing this? Perhaps the sisters were not the harsh tribunal I have believed all these years. Maybe I was the merciless judge who couldn't accept the truth of my own flawed self. Did I attribute my own sense of shame and failure to them, misconstruing it as their judgment of me?

FATHER DE GROOT

When I revisited my journals about Father De Groot, who nursed me through malaria, I was surprised to read that he said that my stay in Muloza had been one of the happiest times for him. Reading those lines I wanted to hug that gentle man, whose solitary days were filled with the loneliness of celibacy in a foreign land.

I then wondered what had happened to him. How long did he stay in Malawi? Was he still alive? An intense need to find out propelled me to search the Internet, where I found the answers I sought.

Father De Groot died in the Netherlands in 2002 at the age of seventy-seven. Born in 1925, he had entered the minor seminary at fourteen. I wondered if our two weeks together were the only time in his life when he had shared the pleasant companionship of a woman.

As I looked at his obituary photo and read the eulogy, I broke down and sobbed. That amazing man had served in Malawi for forty-seven years in nine different missions, many of which he built, along with a large secondary school for girls. "One of the great builders of the diocese . . . worked to improve the living conditions of the people in the villages . . . creating water projects and improving the status of women . . . He lost his heart to Malawi. While his body was dying in the Netherlands, his soul was still in Africa."

Reading Father De Groot's eulogy, I felt the sharp poignancy of having spent time with him without any sense of who he truly was. I just took him at face value. Though very grateful for his care, I left him that last day with little grasp on how significantly our lives had touched—or how he might have felt when I left.

Tears flowed on and off the afternoon I first read his obituary: over his loss and my regret that my search for him had not come sooner. I might have written to him, let him know that he was not forgotten by that young nun of twenty-eight for whom he had so tenderly cared.

But—hidden in the afternoon of tears—an emotion far deeper and darker surfaced. As I read about his astounding years of meaningful service to the people of Malawi, first envy, then anger, rose in me. He had lived the life I had envisioned for myself—a life I felt was taken from me.

FATHER PRINSEN

Writing this memoir prompted me to learn what became of Father Prinsen, our renowned Likulezi teacher. I was surprised to read on the Internet that he left Likulezi in mid-1971, a month or two after I was sent home. Why did he leave? He had been there less than two years. Did the upheaval in the missionary subculture created by our group of young priests and nuns splash any blame on him as our teacher? Or were there any consequences for him over that false and bizarre rumor that I was being kicked out of Malawi by the president because of something I had done with him?

He died at eighty-three in the Netherlands on Easter Day 2011—just months before I searched for him. I wish I could have thanked him for all he taught me . . . and asked him why he left Likulezi when he did.

PILOT PROJECT COMPANIONS

The Pilot Project was a grand experiment that proved its central thesis: the value of a cultural orientation program for newly arrived sisters. The five of us in the project developed warm, personal ties with Malawians, an ability to speak the language, an empathetic understanding of Malawian culture, and a meaningful engagement with it. We achieved in nine months what many of the Dutch sisters working there for years had not.

Yet the overall outcome of the Project proved to be damaging for almost everyone involved. All the potential concerns noted in the planning phase became reality, and the five younger sisters, as well as the older Dutch community, were traumatized by the events of those years. I, along with three of the other four in the Pilot Project, left MMS after that experience. Only Yoli has remained a Medical Mission Sister up to the present time. The other three—Norma, Pat, and Flora—left Malawi of their own choice within the next year. I was the only one who bore the stigma of having been exiled.

In 2012 we four ex-MMS had a reunion after years of little or no contact. For three days we wallowed in the joy of our renewed friendships and discovered the diverse journeys each had traveled since leaving Malawi. As the days passed we slowly peeled back the bandages covering forty-year-old wounds. We found healing in speaking and listening to what each of us still carried inside from that crucible period in our young lives. Older now, we were able to reflect on that period of upheaval and the forces at work in the Malawian missionary culture of the 1970s. We acknowledged that we were forever changed as individuals by that "best of times, worst of times" African sojourn.

As we talked nonstop during our waking hours, we kept bumping up against the lapses and discrepancies in our memories of that shared time. Major events were forgotten by one or the other; even photos weren't able to spark a memory. Time frames and people were a hodgepodge of differently remembered details. The other three were grateful that I had kept some mementos, since they had lost or couldn't locate their photos, journals, and letters. It became obvious that I was the one needing to resurrect our story and heal from the telling of it.

MALAWI

Malawi is known as the Warm Heart of Africa because of its people. Forty years have elapsed since this small nation was the second poorest country in the world. There has been little substantive improvement in the poverty level, and AIDS has decimated my beloved people of the Lower Shire Plain.

GERARD

In the months and years following my departure from Malawi, my superego's minions, like little scavenger mice, chewed on the facts of my relationship with Gerard and tore them into shreds, leaving a pile of evidence that he was the cause of my exile. In its role of protecting my ego, memory revised the actual events into a story that made me an innocent victim who resisted Gerard's overtures. Because I couldn't bear to acknowledge my part in the relationship, our intimate times together, or my expressions of love to him—those facts had been whisked away. Deceptive memory repressed whatever didn't fit my self-image, shielding me from the remembrance of my own actions.

During the many months of steeping myself in Gerard's thick pile of long-ago letters, his soul was revealed. I moved from focusing on what his love had cost me, to a rediscovery of the desirable man I had rejected. As I re-met him through his letters and tapes, I fell in love with him afresh and grieved his loss from my life. Tears fell on many pages and regret rose like a chest pain. I longed to have his forgiveness.

As my memoir was nearing publication, I received the news that Gerard had died unexpectedly during routine surgery on July 12, 2013.

SISTER AIMEE

I look back with motherly compassion on that naive young woman who had such huge aspirations but so little of the self-authority needed for making critical choices. As a child and nun she longed to be a saint and thought she could achieve the unachievable—a perfect life. No wonder her self-image and dreams were destroyed in Malawi, where she met criticism and judgment from the other missionaries and confronted her own failures and immaturity. Like so many females, she was driven by the need for acceptance and love. She hadn't learned yet to claim her life as hers alone to choose, to value her innate beauty and worth as a woman, and to accept her feet of clay. That was a long time in coming.

Young Sister Aimee remains nestled deep in my psyche, though I have grown stronger and wiser over the years. Writing this memoir, one truth stands out: when faced with a choice between judgment and compassion—for others or oneself—always choose compassion.

If you, like young Sister Aimee, struggle to find your unique voice in a culture, religion, family, or relationship that makes you doubt your worth and your right to self-determination, I encourage you to trust that deepest voice inside you . . . and may you be blessed with someone who listens and honors that voice.